This book is dedicated to Lorraine, for support and putting up with an endless obsession with history

A Hundred Years On

A Hundred Years On

The Great War and Other
Events on Cannock Chase

By
Christopher John

Birmingham Branch, Western Front
Association
and
Battlefield Guide Badge 32; The Guild of
Battlefield Guides

Reveille
PRESS

Reveille Press is an imprint of
Tommies Guides Military Booksellers & Publishers

Gemini House
136-140 Old Shoreham Road
Brighton
BN3 7BD

www.tommiesguides.co.uk

First published in Great Britain by
Reveille Press 2013

For more information please visit
www.reveillepress.com

© 2013 Christopher John

A catalogue record for this book is available from the
British Library.

ISBN 978-1-908336-59-0

Cover design by Reveille Press

Printed and bound by
Print-on-Demand Worldwide, Peterborough

CONTENTS

PREFACE

THE AUTHOR, Christopher John, is both a member of the Birmingham branch of the Western Front Association and a badged Battlefield Guide (Badge 32) of the International Guild of Battlefield Guides. Having been interested in the Great War since first watching the 1964 television series *The Great War* produced by the BBC for the fiftieth anniversary of the conflict, Christopher began visiting the old Western Front in the early 1990s.

In 2004, Christopher began organising trips to the Western Front for the Birmingham Branch of the Western Front Association. Becoming more interested in telling others about the Great War, he joined the IGBG in 2006, achieving the status of a badged guide in 2008. Christopher has a wide interest in history but particularly the Great War and with a focus on the involvement of, and effects on, the general populations and societies involved.

Both the author and Birmingham branch would encourage readers and groups to visit the sites on the Chase and would be happy to provide a guide for interested parties by prior arrangement.

Contact The Birmingham Branch WFA on:
www.wfa-birmingham.org.uk

FOREWORD

AS THE events of the Great War have passed from living memory and the infamous battlefields and conflict landscapes have changed in appearance, often bearing little resemblance to their wartime state, it is vitally important that they are remembered and documented, in order that generations to come will understand the momentous events that shaped our modern world.

There are many unsung-heroes, people and places that played intrinsic roles in the events of nearly 100 years ago but often they are in danger of passing unnoticed and unrecorded.

In this booklet, Chris John has taken one such place, which is special to us in the West Midlands, and placed it in the context of the many young soldiers from different continents who passed through its windswept and beautiful landscape on their way to experience the horrors of 'the war to end all wars'.

Chris, a fully qualified Battlefield Guide, has looked at the history, examined the archaeology and walked the ground, ensuring that his descriptions and narrative are rich in colour and detail. This book offers a fascinating insight into a little known yet hugely significant feature of our local history.

Jonathan Dale
Chairman Western Front Association (Birmingham Branch)

INTRODUCTION

FOR THOSE of us with an interest in history and past events, visiting the actual sites where historical events took place usually enhances our understanding and perception of them. Sometimes, if we are lucky, there is a tangible remnant from the past to help us in our understanding. The remains of a Roman villa, a medieval castle's towers, stone walls and dungeons, perhaps earth works such as the massive Iron Age ditches around Maiden Castle. Other objects such as the wooden walls of HMS Victory that ensured Britain's pre-eminent place as ruler of the seas for a hundred years, the steel walls of HMS Belfast, its radar that helped to track the Scharn-horst to its watery grave also embody the essence of history.

But more often the site no longer shows distinct signs of its previous history. Bosworth and Naseby are agricultural fields. Visit the Western Front in France and Flanders today and there is no obvious sign of the vast network of trenches that sheltered the several hundred thousand men of the opposing armies, a few hundred yards apart for four years. But the traces are there. Few surface signs perhaps, but advances in archaeology, particularly the science of geophysics, allow us a glimpse back in time before formal excavation reveals the deeper tracts of the past. Other indications may come from the study of many sources such as old records and maps or aerial photography. But a general truism may be that with the passage of time the ground softens and changes, and generally surface traces of past events disappear and with them the memory of the importance of what took place.

Cannock Chase is typical of this and this book is primarily aimed at imparting an understanding of what occurred there across the first six decades of the twentieth century. During that time, our society changed irrevocably as armed conflict and total war changed the perception and organisation, not once but twice, of who we were and how we live as a nation. Nowadays, on a Sunday morning, the Chase appears wild, populated by walkers and mountain bikers. No obvious remains are there, no decayed huts or buildings, little to suggest that a hundred years ago several thousand young men lived and trained there at any one time, preparing to participate in the first great industrial war, from which many would not return.

These events involved the Chase to a large degree. I hope two themes will run through these pages: how events far away caused such significant change upon the Chase and how events there, such as the training and supplying of reinforcements, particularly to the New Zealand Rifle Brigade, in turn affected the outcome of the monumental struggles abroad.

There are other sites of historical interest at the Chase, too; differing aspects of the Great War, German cemeteries, RAF Hednesford and the Katyn Wood Memorial. But more importantly, attempts have been made to set them in their proper context. This book is not an effort to give the reader a full guide of the site, or a complete account of the building of the training camps there, as this has been covered already elsewhere. Rather, this book's purpose is to give an overall understanding of what and who were there and the context of their importance in historical events. By exploring the Chase in this manner, the area becomes as a place of great historical significance and such memories should always be kept alive.

CHAPTER 1

CHANGES IN HISTORY AND THEIR EFFECTS ON THE CHASE

MANY PLACES in the heart of the country claim to be the geographical centre of England, furthest from the sea in any direction. The Area of Outstanding Natural Beauty at Cannock Chase, Staffordshire, can lay as good a claim as any to be the holder of that distinction. To its north, moorlands stretch up into the Peak District and the foothills of the Pennines roll away towards Scotland. Westwards lies Wales with its idyllic hills and mountains. Eastwards, the land is mainly agricultural, eventually settling into the flatlands of East Anglia. South of the area now lies the Birmingham/Wolverhampton city conurbation, which finally gives way to agriculture lands again, eventually leading to the south coast. Surrounded by small towns, Stafford, Rugeley, Lichfield and Cannock, the area has been one of untouched land and moor throughout history.

Watling Street, the famous Roman road, skirted its southern borders. South of Lichfield was Wall, an important Imperial staging post on the route, but no major roads, Roman or later, cut across the high wastes of the Chase. Mercian Saxon kings, perhaps even the great Offa, may have hunted across it. There was also murder and mayhem, as three years ago, in the south eastern corner of the area, the Staffordshire Hoard was uncovered. It is a collection of hastily buried treasure, bits and pieces of Saxon gold mainly of a military nature. Golden sword hilts, intricately worked patterns inlaid with jewels, and most intriguingly, a thin gold cross, a symbol of the new religion sweeping the land, perhaps ripped from where it adorned the front binding of a rare book, hastily folded and stuffed into a pocket or bag. The decorated solid gold-hinged cheek protector piece, broken from a magnificent chieftain's helmet was also found amongst the hoard. All collected and then hastily buried, by whom, and what happened to them yet to be discovered? Disaster must have swiftly overwhelmed them in their turn, as they never came back and their booty lay buried across the centuries.

Other great disturbances came and went. The Wars of the Roses saw nothing to trouble the Chase. The English Civil War, the great struggle between Charles I, convinced that he was a king appointed and anointed by God's will, and his querulous parliament, saw troubled times with some events around the edge of the Chase. In 1642, King Charles' royalist army passed across the north of the Chase from Derby to Stafford, moving onto Shrewsbury before swinging back eastwards and meeting the Parliamentarian army at the Battle of Edgehill in Warwickshire.

The struggle did involve men of Cannock, namely the miners. For the district by now had a reputation for the simple and dangerous coal mining of the times and the miners were summoned, either for money, love of the cause or at the muzzle of a pistol, to perform a crucial act in the second siege of Lichfield cathedral – to reclaim the fortified Cathedral Close for the Royalist cause. It involved tunnelling and laying the only explosive mine in English history. Something that coincidently in years to come would link them with the tunnellers of Messines, whose work in 1917 would be commemorated by the New Zealand Rifle Brigade at Brocton Camp. Deep coalmining from large collieries survived into the late twentieth century.

At Cannock, troubled times in England had barely touched the area, so surely events in foreign lands would have no repercussions here? But by the beginning of the twentieth century, foreign events would indeed unleash a flood whose waves would reach even this wild and little touched area. For the first sixty years of the twentieth century would see thousands of men brought to the Chase for military training. First, in 1914, came masses of excited volunteers all keen to 'do their bit'. Later, as the casualty toll at the front became heavier and heavier, the rush of volunteers dwindled and finally ceased. Reluctant conscripts were forced into service by the Military Service Act of 1916 and duly took their place. To house them, two large hutted military training camps were built. To service them, roads were laid down and railways constructed into the camps. Provision for necessary water and electric supply as well as sewerage and drainage also had to be made. No wonder local historians CJ and GP Whitehouse entitled their book on the camps *A Town for Four Winters* (Hereafter referred to as *A Town*). Infantry training took place, practice trenches were dug and rifle ranges were built, while sacks were hung from gantries for bayonet practice.

The pace of war soon quickened and two further groups of men arrived on the Chase, both from opposite sides of the conflict, with one group quite literally coming half way around the world to join the war. The first of these disparate groups were German Prisoners of War captured in France and Flanders and now to be accommodated in a part of the camp converted for the purpose. The second were men from New Zealand, who as the 5th Battalion The New Zealand Rifle Brigade took over the camp in 1917 and became responsible for its administration and the training of both their own reinforcements and any other British units stationed there.

Ironically, both these groups would leave a permanent reminder of their presence there in one of the few Commonwealth War Graves Commission cemeteries built on British soil, far distant from the several thousand others scattered across Europe and the world. For both would suffer from one of the great, but now largely unremembered, tragedies of the early twentieth century, one that probably killed more worldwide than the previous four years of fighting; the deadly Spanish flu pandemic that swept around the world, reaching England in the autumn and winter of 1918. Now these men lie in the same military cemetery; British, New Zealanders and Germans, all soldiers of armies united by their fate. The New Zealanders, as with the Anglo-Saxon hoard, also left a buried treasure behind, one that is now coming to be recognised as being of increasing historical and military importance. In the only known example of its kind within the UK, they created in concrete, complete with trench lines and defences, a scale model of one of their most famous battles; the storming of the village of Messines in Belgium, part of the Battle of Messiness, which began on the 7th June 1917. Used for 'topographical instruction' the model stayed on as a tourist attraction into the 1930s until the site was abandoned and forgotten during the Second World War.

Now, with the site re-discovered, the model is increasingly recognised as a site of *'national or even international importance'* (Joint MoD and Staffs CC archaeological survey 2008). It is the only known survivor of its kind, built by men who were there at the time. The New Zealanders also left behind another reminder of their brigade, the grave of Freda their Great Dane mascot. Legend has it she was found in France and brought back to England and died there in 1918. Today there is a headstone marking her grave that was erected and is looked after by the Friends of Cannock Chase.

Further south of the Visitors Centre is another Great War site built not for the training of soldiers but for their recovery from the physical and mental wounds sustained during their service. Brindley Heath Military Hospital is a hutted establishment with several wards all adjoining a long central corridor. Accommodation for the hospital staff, the RAMC doctors, QARANC sisters and nurses as well as VADs and orderlies also had to be provided.

After the 'War to End Wars'

At last, in 1918, the longed for Armistice and peace arrived. "Après la Guerre finis, soldat Anglais partir" as the French and British sang in the estaminets behind the lines of the Western Front. Training ceased and battalions in residence were largely shipped out to become Occupation Forces in Germany. By May 1919, only the New Zealand Rifle Brigade and the German prisoners within their camp were left on the Chase. The NZRB held a formal ceremony with Stafford civic dignitaries, exchanged flags and colours and then left for repatriation. Except for the PoW section, the camp was empty. Soon, under the terms of the agreement of use, work was contracted for its demolition. Surplus equipment and huts were offered for sale, the railway was torn up, the famous landmarks such as the four generator house chimneys and the huge water tank all came down. The huts had not stood on concrete floors or foundations, so gradually nature re-asserted herself; the outlines of the camps softened and, like an old soldier, faded away.

Only the rows of lonely crosses at the cemetery remained, and of course, the model of Messines. With its own guardian in a small tin hut, it was left for the curious and idle to look at and wonder for the price of one or two old pence. The Hospital remained as a Ministry of Pensions hospital; there were many old miners around with varying degrees of pneumoconiosis, miners' lung; 'the Dust'. After the 1920s, it had a further use as a home for miners and was converted into Brindley Miners' Village.

By 1930, the Chase had reverted to its former wild nature. However, far away events were again unfolding that would have deep consequences for the Chase. By the late 1930s, re-armament was in the air. A new power rose on the far off continent, one that again troubled the peace of the land. It was obvious the nation must once again look to its defences. For the same reason the Chase again seemed a suitable place for a large training camp as it was close to roads and had particularly good rail access.

This time it would be the Royal Air Force rather than the army that would establish a facility here. Behind the area now occupied by the Visitor Centre work started on RAF Hednesford. It would not be an airfield but a training centre for ground crews, riggers and mechanics, all of whom would be required in increasing numbers. Large instructional hangars were built and small aircraft could be flown in, landing on the sports field and taxiing into the hangars to be used as instructional airframes. Accommodation huts, messes and cookhouses, just as in the First war, all had to be built with connecting services such as roads, water pipes, power supplies and drainage. Most loved of all by the Chief Warrant Officer, a large parade ground occupied the centre of the camp. Then, in the 1950s, it would undertake two further important duties, as we shall see.

The camp is now gone and little remains of the site. But with a map, and orientated by one or two landmarks, the layout of the camp can still be made out. With that in mind, one can now safely commit that most heinous of RAF crimes, one that would have had the Chief Warrant Officer crimson with rage, screaming exactly what he thought of you across the camp. One can walk directly across the parade ground instead of around it! Nobody set foot on an RAF parade ground – unless parading or undertaking training and Heaven help you if you did!!

In the 1960s came the final permanent change to this part of the Chase, the establishment of the German Military Cemetery. After both wars burials of German service personnel and civilian internees were scattered across the country nearest to wherever they had died, or their bodies had been discovered. For better keeping and maintenance of the graves it was felt that gathering as many as possible into a single site would be preferable.

The Chase was chosen for ease of access and the fact that there was a nearby CWGC cemetery meant that maintenance could be easily contracted in. But some suggest there was another reason; that the landscape, especially in winter, is rather bleak and Germanic in appearance. Work commenced in the last years of the 1950s and early 1960s and today two war cemeteries exist in close proximity; Cannock Chase War Cemetery with direct connections to the use of the Chase, and the German cemetery without direct connections, but still with many interesting stories to tell.

There is one more memorial on the Chase, dedicated to an event long ago and far away. The Katyn Wood massacre, carried out on Stalin's orders, saw the killing of a swathe of the Polish officer and professional classes during the Second World War. The Memorial is set in the woods on the Chase, as a large Polish community stayed on in the area after the war, erected in memory of their murdered citizens and so the world should not forget this dreadful crime.

By the end of the 1960s, military activity had at last ceased on Cannock Chase. Now it is difficult to find traces of that time but they are there for those who know where to look. I hope this guide might help the visitor in seeking out those traces and understanding some of the events that took place over fifty years of the last century and the important part this area played in them.

CHAPTER 2

THE SUMMER OF 1914, EVENTS FAR OFF AND FAR AWAY

T HE FIRST World War was a result of simmering European tensions stretching back sixty years to the 1850s and the rise of the German state of Prussia as the major military power of Western and Central Europe. Prussia went to war three times to establish itself as the pre-eminent rising state of the time. Wars against Austro-Hungary and poor little Denmark in the 1860s broke it free from the Hapsburg Empire and gave it access to build a naval waterway, the Kiel Canal, from the Baltic to the North Sea. Something that Britain would come to see as one of the greatest threats to its national security.

But its greatest military achievement was the crushing and humiliating defeat of Emperor Louis Napoleon's France in the Franco-Prussian War of 1870-71. Britain had stayed neutral in all these conflicts, even facilitating the Peace Treaty of London at the end of the Franco-Prussian War. However, Anglo-German relationships were never warm. Kaiser Wilhelm II, although deeply in thrall of his British Grandmother, Queen Victoria, did not get on well with his Uncle Bertie, later to be King Edward VII. Deeply mistrusted, not helped by bombastic anti-British pronouncements from the all-highest at regular intervals, relations went from bad to worse with the German ambition to build a large navy centred on the Baltic. As the dominant naval power in the region, indeed in the world, Britain perceived that as a direct threat. Germany already had the largest, most professional and most feared army in Europe. Why else would it need a large navy except to challenge British dominance on the seas around Europe?

As a result of the European problems a web of intrigue began to spin that would tie two disparate fractions into opposing military camps, the members of each bound by secret treaties to come to each other's aid in time of war. Despite its war for independence, Germany's main and natural ally was the Austro-Hungarian Hapsburg Empire. Britain and France, although traditionally old adversaries, drew closer, particularly due to Edward VIIs love of France and his rapport with its people and government. The Entente Cordial came into being. The Russian Empire also came into the fold. Its ruler, Tsar Nicholas II, another grandson of Queen Victoria and cousin of both the Kaiser and King George V, saw Russia as a protector of the Slavic people of the Balkans, particularly Serbia, who was fearful of annexation and repression by Austro-Hungary. With all the major powers tied to one side or the other by treaty, events in 1914 began to gather momentum and take on an almost self-fulfilling destiny, leading inexorably towards war.

In Britain, the summer of 1914 was warm and pleasant. The usual social round, the London season, took place. On Derby Day, King George V, the only British Monarch ever to have set foot on Indian soil as its Emperor, joined his people on Epsom Downs to see the appropriately named Durbar II win the Derby. Photos of the day show large crowds, tented shows and booths, pearly kings and queens; this was a Londoners holiday day out. Many watched the race from the upper decks of parked open topped London buses. Nobody could possibly imagine that within five months those same buses would be ferrying British troops to war in France.

Their world began to change forever in June 1914. Far away in Sarajevo, a young Serbian nationalist, Gavrilo Princip, sought to further his cause by assassinating the heir to the Austro-Hungarian throne, Archduke Franz Ferdinand, and his wife, Princess Sophia. Three or four pistol shots can be said to have changed Europe more profoundly than the combined efforts of many kings and emperors beforehand. Austro-Hungary saw a chance to humiliate and annex Serbia. It issued an ultimatum demanding Serbia disarm and in effect surrender to immediate Hapsburg rule. Serbia gave in to most of the terms immediately but Austro-Hungary wanted war against Serbia. The response was stated to be insufficient and the Hapsburg Empire mobilised to attack.

By now, the deadly game of move and counter move had begun to gather an unstoppable momentum. Russia, seeking to protect fellow Slavs, threatened mobilisation of its vast armies if Serbia was attacked. If Russia attacked Austro-Hungary, Germany would be bound to come to the Hapsburgs' aid. In turn, if Russia entered the war France and possibly Britain were honour bound to support her.

Nobody in Britain, or on the continent, had foreseen such drastic events happening so suddenly. To the amazement of most, the joy of many and the despair of a few, the happy summer of 1914, so recently expressed at Derby Day, was suddenly spiralling out of control towards a major European war.

But even now there were many, even in government, who could see no need for British involvement. If war came it would be a continental conflict, a clash of vast armies to which

Britain's small land forces could play little part. At most, possibly some naval support might be appropriate. But in the first days of August came a move by Germany that guaranteed to draw Britain into the imminent war. Germany had long foreseen that it was trapped between two opposing powers, Russia in the east and France to the west. To cope with a possible war on two fronts they had adopted a plan proposed by a staff officer, General Schlieffen, in the 1890s. The aim of the Schlieffen Plan was to knock France out quickly before turning all possible force on 'the Russian Steamroller' as it was optimistically called. To do that, German armies would sweep into France along its furthest northeastern border, with the aim of encircling Paris. If Paris surrendered quickly then all force could be turned eastwards against the Tsar's Armies, who meanwhile would only be opposed by a small holding force.

There was however one major flaw in the plan. To attack Northern France the German Army must have passage across neutral Belgium, either by agreement or by invasion. Belgium was an artificial country created eighty years earlier as a neutral buffer between France and Germany, precisely to prevent that form of aggression. Furthermore, there were three main guarantors of Belgian independence by treaty; Germany, France, and Britain.

By the first days of August, all sides had mobilised for war, regular armies were ready and reservists had been called back to their regiments with all possible haste. On August 4th the blow fell. Germany demanded the Belgian government grant free passage for her armies across her territory. The Belgians, under their king, Leopold, hesitated and then made their momentous decision. Passage would not be granted and any attempt at invasion would be resisted militarily, tiny though the Belgian Army might be. Britain issued an ultimatum to the Kaiser and the German government. Any attempt to compromise Belgian independence and force an armed passage through her territory would be considered an act of war contrary to the treaty that created Belgium. If so, Britain would be obliged to enter the war to maintain that independence.

Anxiously awaiting the German government's response to their ultimatum, the British foreign secretary, Lord Edward Grey, gazed out on the gas lit streets of London and made his famous melancholic pronouncement.

> "The lamps are going out all over Europe, we shall not see them lit again in our lifetime".

The final notes of the prelude were fading away, signalling the end of Victorian and Edwardian Britain and Europe.

CHAPTER 3

THE RUSH TO ENLIST AND THE CANNOCK CHASE RESERVE CENTRE

S O FAR, the reader may be wondering when exactly we might get to some description and detail of events on the Chase itself. The preceding chapters have been an attempt to put the momentous changes that occurred at the Chase into historical context and perspective. The world events that led up to the changes of use from 1914 swept even into this quiet corner in the middle of England. So great was their scale internationally that for the first time even this wild and untouched area would be troubled by the prospect and preparations for war.

The outbreak of hostilities was met, not as one might have expected, by dismay, but astonishingly by scenes of almost religious fervour and rejoicing across the capital cities of Europe. In all countries, crowds gathered cheering and singing patriotic songs. Civilians of all nationalities waved and cheered, embraced and threw flowers at troops departing for the front, wherever that might turn out to be.

One unexpected phenomenon in Britain was the sudden

rush of men to enlist in the army. Britain did not have a history of widespread military service. On the continent a form of compulsory national service and army training followed by several years on the Reserve ensured armies of several million men could quickly be raised. But Britain had a small professional volunteer army, backed up by the Territorial battalions initially created for home service. At any time, about half the regular army was stationed abroad in the vast Empire. Under the terms of the Entente Cordial, two army corps, almost 90,000 men, would be sent to France as the British Expeditionary Force (BEF), a small contribution against the armies of two to three million each that France and Germany were expected to raise, and the even larger armies of Austro-Hungary and Russia. Prompted by the fear that the 'war might be over by Christmas' and by patriotic fervour to do their duty, men rushed to the recruiting offices in unprecedented numbers.

On the outbreak of war, Field Marshall Lord Horatio Herbert Kitchener was appointed Minister of War. A thoroughly professional and experienced soldier, Lord Kitchener realised that the war would not be over by Christmas; indeed it was not likely to be over for some considerable time. Therefore, a large expansion of the army would be necessary, over and above the numbers already pressing forward. As early as August, in probably the first modern use of propaganda, the famous poster was issued. Lord Kitchener staring with piercing eyes, over a walrus moustache with his finger pointing directly at the viewer; *"Your country needs YOU"*. He had hoped for 100,000 volunteers for his planned New Army (K1) battalions. Within a week he had them but the flood did not stop there.

K1 was followed by K2 the 'second hundred thousand' and even K3 before the patriotic rush began to falter.

Within a few months, nearly a million men are thought to

have volunteered or to have been called from the reserve to the Colours. The organisation for accepting such numbers, mustering them into battalions of regiments, each battalion a thousand men strong, was exceptional. Imagine, each new soldier would require a khaki serge uniform and cap complete with metal buttons, regimental shoulder and cap badges. Each man would also require, at the government's expense, standard underwear, socks and especially a pair of boots, a million left and a million right to be manufactured, unless some very strange recruits had got through the process!

Even so, many Tommies would swear they had two left boots until they were broken in and comfortable. Each man would require a knife, fork and spoon, tin mug and alloy mess tin. A greatcoat, a pack, the dreaded pair of puttees; the list of full kit seems endless. Above all, as an infantryman, a short magazine Lee-Enfield rifle and accompanying bayonet and scabbard complete with ammunition to be carried in webbing pouches was also a necessity. For each New Army battalion, officers had to found. Retired majors and colonels were dragged back to camp. Public schoolboys with some training in the Officers Training Corps at school were eagerly sought as subalterns. Experienced ex-NCOs were even more keenly sought after. All would have to train and learn together, probably for the next year, before they could reach the standard required to take their part in any form of co-ordinated military activity.

Above all, the War Office had an even greater problem, where to house and train the New Army until it was ready to depart for service overseas. The practical considerations of where several hundred thousand men were going to sleep, keep warm and dry, eat and wash were considerable and needed to be met before their military training could even begin. There were nowhere near enough permanent barracks, as large numbers of troops had not traditionally been kept within the UK, and certainly not in England, so new but temporary facilities were urgently required. Thus, at last, we come to the establishment on the Chase of two large military establishments: Brocton and Rugeley camps, jointly to be entitled the Cannock Chase Reserve Centre, in early 1915.

CJ and GP Whitehouse cover the building of the camps and the landscape engineering in some detail in their book *A Town for Four Winters* and this book is not an attempt to duplicate that. Accordingly, it will make little reference to the establishment of the camps. Instead, this book is more an interpretation, one which aims to set the existence of the Cannock Chase Reserve Centre into its historical context and to look in a little more detail at some specific aspects of the camp and its archaeology as well as some of the visible record that remains. One of the dominant themes is why events so far away and abroad so deeply affected this remote and quiet area of England to the great extent that they did.

The area fulfilled the necessary requirements for a military training area. It was remote and covered a large area of open land with little surrounding civilian occupation to complain of noise or disturbance. There were also road connections, with the main A5 not too far away. But most important of all, particularly in the railway age, there was good rail access to the north and south of the camp. A military railway system, known as 'The Tackeroo Railway', not a colonial name but one predating the camp by many years, was constructed from these main lines into the centre of both camps and out again. All goods, food, stores, coal, ammunition etc would be delivered into the stores' cuttings and sidings. Men would not be. They disembarked from the train at the nearest station and marched to the camp.

The plans of the camps can be seen from existing maps now displayed on the Internet, at the excellent Staffs Past

Postcard of early days at Brocton. Huts completed, training in trench digging in foreground. Landmarks of water tank and power house chimneys visible on skyline.

Track site. The layout of the camps looks rather primitive and a little chaotic. Such had been the rush to construction that no attempt had been made to lay out roads and track ways. Rugeley Camp had various blocks of huts, perhaps twenty to a block, a huge fire hazard should one have broken out. Brocton camp was strung out along Chase road, stores and administrative buildings and the railway are to the east of the road, the huts in groups of four sit along the west side. Photos of the camps give a clear indication of their appearance; relentless wooden barrack huts, many at differing angles, in a very open and treeless landscape, very different to today where scrub and small trees have generally taken over. The images confirm doors opened mainly onto plain ground with no effort at constructed roads or pathways between the huts.

Perhaps the only area at Brocton where some effort at a conventional layout was made was at the H lines to the north. Maybe this area was constructed last or later, more on a small grid pattern with two main tracks dividing hut groups and a small parade ground. Not surprisingly, this is the only area today where traces of the old roadways and layouts can be clearly seen both on the ground, as well as on the satellite photos available on Google Earth. Here can also be seen some of the training earthworks associated with the camp. The plans do not show significant parade grounds, as training was to be mainly practical and conducted on the surrounding moorland.

The most important aspects of training can be seen via a simple statistic; the number of rifle ranges that were constructed near to Rugeley Camp. This was a place primarily for infantry training and the main requirements of the infantryman were the accurate and efficient firing of his Lee-Enfield rifle and the ready use of the bayonet attached to the muzzle. *A Town* notes the construction of 6 different ranges, the largest a monster with a massive central stop butt of sand and gravel, capable of holding 90 targets. Deep in the woods the stop butt is still there and broken copper bullet jackets and pieces of lead can still be found. On the photos of the camp other activity can be seen; practice trenches are being dug and trestles and gallows can be seen with suspended sacks hanging from them; the instruments of bayonet training. Rush forward with a screaming yell, plunge the sharpened bayonet deep into the belly of the enemy, then twist and withdraw rushing on to the next victim!

What was the nature of the work of the reserve centre? Both camps had been erected in a rush when the need to suddenly house hundreds of thousands of volunteers, recalled reservists and regular army battalions returned from overseas service, was at its most pressing. The New Army battalions of K1, K2, and K3 would need full training both for their men and their officers. Perhaps it was envisaged that camps such as Brocton and Rugeley would take a role in such training, but it is unclear if they did. By the end of 1915, many Kitchener battalions were moving to France to gain front line battle experience. Some of the first K1 battalions saw action as early as at the Battle of Loos, in September 1915. But all would have left the United Kingdom to undertake their roles in the first great British offensive, the battle of the Somme, in July 1916.

The real purpose of the camps was as the name implied, the training of reserve forces for the various battalions with a presence there. These would be later volunteers, soldiers returning to active service, often after being ill or wounded and increasingly, after late 1916, conscripts undergoing compulsory military service. The Military Act of 1916 deemed all fit men between the ages of 19 – 41 to be available for service. By 1916, the flow of volunteers had almost dried up. What was needed now were not whole new battalions, as in 1914, but a steady supply of trained replacements for the existing units. The daily casualty figures from the front were a constant drain on manpower. Even without battle the average day saw front line casualties from shellfire, sudden enemy raids, wiring and patrolling No Man's Land at night, sniping, as well as illness, trench fever and trench foot; the causes seemed endless. At regular intervals new drafts of men would be requested from the training centres and duly dispatched to France and Flanders. Such men would receive their training on the Chase; musketry at the rifle ranges, bayonet practice on the hanging sacks, Mills bomb training, basic trench layout and digging practice, as well as a host of others.

It is no surprise that the list of units known to have been resident on the Chase, and quoted in *A Town,* are all Reserve (Training) battalions, many of whom were regiments of Northern Command, under whose jurisdiction the camp originally came. Other units in residence were mainly Young Soldier's battalions. These were formed to hold and train 18 year old conscripts whilst they waited to reach the age of 19 and become eligible for active service. Also held at the Chase were other more experienced young soldiers. Enlistment into the army had been open to those aged 18 or over. The rush to volunteer in 1914 had seen many younger volunteers pretend to be 18. Some had been close at 17, but often they were just 16 years or younger. Many were weeded out by the rigours of physical training but some had survived to become front line soldiers. However, the army had been rather embarrassed by parents continually seeking MPs' help and generally making a nuisance of themselves, as the army saw it, in trying to get underage volunteers released. To counter this, the age of front line service was set as 19 years, but was still not generally enforced. It was not until 1917 that a strict trawl through of units in France was undertaken and anyone found to be under that age, some of them by now front line soldiers of some considerable experience, were returned home to kick their heels in such units, until they reached the eligible age. Again, the list of units on the Chase shows a considerable number of these battalions.

By 1917, the camps and their activities were fully established.

However, with falling recruitment it is likely that, even with the numbers of conscripts, several areas of the camp were not in regular use and several photos show huts with doors open and empty looking windows with no evidence of occupation visible. The availability of accommodation at the camps led to a new twist in the story of the Great War on Cannock Chase; the arrival of two further groups of men from overseas and from opposing sides of the conflict; German Prisoners of War and the New Zealand Rifle Brigade.

CHAPTER FOUR

MEN FROM FAR AWAY – THE BROCTON GERMAN PRISONER OF WAR CAMP

THE NEED to accommodate German Prisoners of War grew steadily from 1916 onwards. Up until then, the British took relatively few prisoners, as the main battles involving the British in 1915 were small scale compared to the titanic struggles that were to come. 1915 saw the Battles of Neuve Chappelle, Festubert, the abortive disaster of Aubers Ridge and in September, the Battle of Loos. None were successful, no gains in terms of territory were made and very few prisoners were taken. The Somme saw some change in that but again the numbers were not large. The film *The Battle of the Somme*, shot by Geoffrey Malins, the official cinematographer, shows scenes of German prisoners being escorted down from the front. The numbers were not high, but they did significantly increase as the Somme battles ground on.

For instance, Edmund Blunden, in his wonderful account of the time, *Undertones of War,* reports the capture of the huge underground German tunnel complex at St Pierre Divion complete with 2,000 occupants, on the edge of the Thiepval plateau in November 1916.

Most Prisoners of War were sent back to Britain. As the need for accommodation grew, a search began for places to establish the PoW camps. Brocton camp was considered suitable as it was isolated away from nearby towns and areas of habitation. All the facilities of a major camp were present, with good road and rail communication and by mid 1916 accommodation was also available as the first rush of volunteers and their need for training was now over. Sources such as *A Town* quote the conversion of the most northerly areas, A and B hut lines, into such a camp. It would be relatively easy to fence off two sections of the camp, build watchtowers and there was ready-made accommodation for prisoners and their guards as well.

A guard would have to be established and the Royal Defence Corps would usually provided this. The Corps consisted of existing Home Service (Garrison) battalions, largely made up of men not up to the physical standards required for front line service. Also included were those wounded who could not return to active service, older regulars too old or not up to standard and so on. Although the Corps was a wartime formation, it remained in service until the mid 1930s and there would have been a guard detachment at Brocton, and confirming this there is one member buried in the war cemetery.

The NZRB history refers to around 2000 Prisoners of War being held in the Camp at Brocton. From the New Zealand history the prisoners would appear to have been well behaved. Postcards found on various websites show the German prisoners engaged in that most popular PoW activity – amateur dramatics, and well-staged shows were apparently a regular feature. The history only refers to one untoward incident. A date is not given but the prisoners seen to have staged a minor protest, probably over rationing. The 5th Battalion turned out to assist the guard and the history records the compound was covered by rifles and two machine guns were trained on the main gates. At this the protest seems to have rapidly faded away.

By the war's end, many prisoners worked on parole on local farms on a daily basis and made a valuable contribution to local agriculture, replacing the men lost to conscription and active service. Once the Armistice was agreed, it appears that the Allies were not as quick to release their prisoners as the Germans were. The Fatherland was suffering famine and starvation, largely as a result of the Royal Navy's blockade, and was anxious to rid itself of useless mouths to feed. In some cases, camps were opened up and the prisoners turned out. Despite this, German prisoners in France and Britain were not so lucky. Many were kept on well into 1920 and were expected to carry on working. The National Archive's material relating to Brocton's PoWs reveals a petition from the PoWs asking for their release to be speeded up and the prisoners had probably had enough of the cold and bleak Cannock Chase winter weather! The PoW section was the last to leave the Camp late in 1920. The New Zealanders had left in 1919 and at last the military use of this area associated with the Great War was over.

However, not everyone went home. The Cannock War cemetery was also locally known as the German Cemetery due to the large number of German PoW burials there, 'Gerfallen Fur Deutschland' along with the hundred of thousands of their compatriots scattered along the Western Front.

CHAPTER FIVE

MARCHING 'THE PICADILLY' – ENTER THE NEW ZEALANDERS

O NE OF the main aims of this book is to contrast the period of the Great War with the previous, peaceful history of Cannock Chase. Once the war began, activity on the Chase began to reflect events elsewhere, finally drawing both the Chase and the British civilian population into the experience of total War. By late 1915, the Chase had been taken over for the training of troops in the initial rush to the colours. By the end of 1916, volunteer numbers had dwindled and conscription had been introduced to maintain manpower for the army. The camps were now fulfilling their function as a holding and training centre for reserves, readying them for service at the front. But there was still one more resource of fighting men that was to make a significant contribution, the men from overseas – the men of the British Empire.

The first actions of the war; the retreat from Mons, the First Battle of The Marne, the Battle of the Aisne and the First Battle of Ypres, in November 1914, had virtually destroyed the original British Expeditionary Force. Short of men, the British Army called on battalions serving at home and hurriedly recalled the many Regular battalions stationed around the world. On top of these measures, the Territorial Army was mobilised for action. Territorial soldiers could not be compelled to undertake Foreign Service, but in keeping with the spirit of the times, most Territorial battalions volunteered for overseas service. Even so, it would take some time before the Territorials and Kitchener's volunteers would be ready for service.

There was a reservoir of manpower within the Empire that was immediately available to the British Government; the highly trained professional soldiers of the Indian Army. Three Indian Army divisions were hurriedly shipped to France and held the line south of Armienteres, providing half the attacking forces for the early 1915 battles. Elsewhere, the Dominions were also mobilising. Canada had its 1st Division in the line around Ypres by mid 1915, where they stood fast as the French colonial troops alongside them broke and fled during the first use of poison gas by the German Army. A second division was forming to arrive in early 1916, later followed by a third and a fourth, eventually forming the Canadian Corps. Even Britain's smallest independent colony, Newfoundland, contributed a battalion, the Newfoundland Regiment, which was to be so savagely mauled in the early hours of the calamitous first day of the Battle of the Somme.

Further away, Australia and New Zealand immediately declared Britain's struggle to be their struggle and volunteers were called for from both colonies. New Zealand had a much smaller population but provided an initial contingent, the New Zealand Expeditionary Force of over 9000 men, which formed up with the 4th Australian Division. They soon proceeded towards Egypt in 1915 for further training, but were sent on from there as part of the ill-fated expedition to seize the Gallipoli Peninsular. As recruits were trained back home in New Zealand, more units were sent forward until it became possible to form a complete New Zealand Division. Of the four brigades constituting the Division, one was a wartime unit formed in 1915; the New Zealand Rifle Brigade. This consisted of numbers 1 to 4 Battalions NZRB and the 5th (Training) Battalion, which would soon become familiar with Brocton Camp. From Gallipoli, now formed into the Australia and New Zealand Army Corps, the ANZACs headed for France, arriving in mid summer 1916 in time to participate in the later stages of the Battle of the Somme. The New Zealand Division also took part in the Battle of Flers-Courcellette.

By early 1917, the New Zealand Division had been sent north from France into Belgium and was destined to play a full part in the Battle of Messines. Afterwards, the division then remained within the Ypres salient, later taking part in the Third Battle of Ypres, more commonly known as Passchendaele. This infamous battle became a five-month slog in which the British Army struggled to advance, as the battlefield became a sodden morass of mud and flooded shell holes. As many wounded soldiers drowned in the mire as died of their wounds back in the hospitals and casualty clearing stations. In March 1918, the nature of the war finally changed, as the German Spring offensive was launched against the British lines in the area of the Fifth Army, driving the line right back across and behind the old Somme battlefield and then came the Battle of the Lys, which was aimed at capturing Ypres in the north.

The New Zealand Division was one of the few reserve units held by the High Command and on the 23rd March, the first day of the *Kaiserschlacht*. They were hurriedly rushed south and thrown into the battle to halt the German advance.

Finally, the New Zealand Division played a full part in the Last 100 Days – the advance to victory, starting with the offensive centred around Villers-Brettoneux on the 8th August 1918, a day labelled by Ludendorf as *'the black day of the German Army'*. Now almost totally overlooked and forgotten, it was a stunning victory for the British and Empire armies. Accompanied by 400 tanks and supported by over 500 aircraft, British and Empire divisions broke through the enemy lines and advanced 5 to 10 miles in a single day. More importantly, the morale of the German Army finally cracked as ten to fifteen thousand German soldiers threw down their arms and surrendered. From that day on, the German High Command knew the war could not be won.

By the time the New Zealand Rifle Brigade was due to send its training battalion into Brocton camp in September 1917, they were only halfway through this history of toil and sacrifice that would see so many New Zealand soldiers killed and wounded. The 'Official History of the New Zealand Rifle Brigade' is a document full of the pride the New Zealanders felt to support the Motherland. It makes it clear that the New Zealand Division and its Rifle Brigade were tough, battle-

As a morale booster most camps had official bands.

hardened outfits. Their men were strong characters, 'hard men' in today's parlance. There is a sense of an innate superiority over the Germans, both in terms of military prowess and achievements, and definitely in terms of morale. Sadly, at the end of each month appears the butcher's bill (the number of dead and wounded from the Brigade for that month). For just a 6-day period between the 6th -12th June 1917, which includes the Battle of Messines, casualties are given as:

	Killed	Wounded	Missing
Officers	8	26	-
Other ranks	136	649	160

From a brigade of about 4000 men, divided into 4 battalions, nearly a quarter needed replacing after just a single week! The figures for the month of November 1917, the end of the Third Battle of Ypres, were as follows:

	Killed	Wounded	Missing
Officers	1	5	-
Other ranks	40	100	-

The figures for April 1918, when the New Zealand Division was thrown into Fifth Army's line to help stem the momentum of the German Spring Offensive south of the Somme are as follows:

	Killed	Wounded	Missing
Officers	5	12	-
Other ranks	102	357	3

It was the job of Brocton Camp to train and provide reinforcements for these losses. The training officers, the tough instructors back for a three-month break from the front line, the cooks, the clerks, the general camp workers and maintenance corps all were there for the purpose of taking young men from the far side of the world turning them into front line soldiers. The official history, which devotes a separate appendix to the activity of its training battalion, makes it clear how proud the men were that the troops were trained in the most modern techniques of warfare. It also recognises that ideas of trench warfare and tactics had changed by the end of 1917. A well as good infantrymen, there was a need for men trained in more specialist activities, especially scouts, who could reconnoitre No Man's Land safely. These guides would learn the area and then bring parties of men, whether carrying parties or whole battalions, safely through the dark and featureless landscape of the front. Also, bombers, skilled in the accurate use of the now ubiquitous Mills bomb, the British hand grenade, as well as Lewis gunners, greatly increased firepower at platoon and section level. The official history proudly states that of each batch of 100 men ready for the front no less than fifteen would be fully trained specialists of this nature.

And what of the *Piccadilly*? Several photos of the Brigade by Thomas Scales, the New Zealand war photographer, entitled '*performing the Piccadilly march past*' show the 5th Battalion on parade and split into companies. What exactly this was, the author has been unable to establish, but many units both in the British Army and others had a signature march at a fast speed. From the dust raised in the pictures, this appears to be a fast march past, possibly representing the fast movements of walkers in Piccadilly Circus, then as now a major London tourist attraction. Anyone from the camp with a few days leave may well have wanted to head for the capital of the British Empire whilst in England.

The importance of all these Empire contributions would be particularly felt after the war. Most countries saw their involvement and the efforts of their men fighting in their own units as the first steps towards nationhood. For the first time, they were not just units of the British Empire. Their men were not placed piecemeal into British divisions but fought in units of their own country and with their own countrymen. For the first time, they felt they were becoming representative units of their own emerging countries, a feeling that would guide each one towards independent nationhood.

CHAPTER 6

LIFE IN THE CAMP AND THE MODEL OF MESSINES

THE CLEAREST idea of how the camps looked and what life there was like for the thousands of volunteers, young soldiers and conscripts can be gleaned from the postcards of the time, many of which are illustrated in *A Town*. In these can be clearly seen the rather bleak layout, particularly of Brocton Camp and the surrounding open and treeless terrain. But greater detail is provided by the work of an official New Zealand war photographer, Thomas Frederick Scales. Initially, Captain Henry Armitage Sanders had been appointed as New Zealand's first official war photographer with special responsibility for the Western Front and it was shortly afterwards that Scales was appointed as *'Cinema expert for New Zealand units in England'*.

How Thomas Scales, generally known as Tommy, obtained this position with the New Zealand forces is unclear. His service record on enlistment in 1917 shows he was a 27-year-old Londoner living with his wife and two children in Islington. His employer is stated as the Whitehead Aeroplane Company but his profession is given as 'cinematographer'. Involved in news filming since a young man, he had been one of the first cameramen to film the war. In 1914, while working for Pathé in a manner similar to that described by Geoffrey Malins in his book *How I Filmed the War,* he had been sent to Belgium and told to get as much action footage as he could. Like Malins, he had accompanied the Belgian Army in its retreat back towards Nieuport, filming there in constant danger as the front established itself. Later in the war he seemed to have given up active cinematography, perhaps he had joined the aircraft factory for, unlike Malins, he was a married man with two children. However, the opportunity to be attached to the New Zealand Division may have seemed too good to miss.

In early 1917, he was enlisted into the New Zealand Army Service Corps as a Private in the role mentioned above. By 1918, he had been promoted to staff sergeant and appears to have been receiving special service pay. He remained in his post for the remainder of the war, visiting and photographing life in the various camps occupied by New Zealand forces. He was discharged in England in late 1919, having attended and photographed victory parades both in London and Paris. He stayed in the cinematography profession, becoming an assistant editor of British Movietone News in the 1930's, involved in producing a weekly cinema newsreel. He retired in the 1950s when he and his wife moved to settle in Cornwall. Sadly, he died shortly afterwards, in 1958, following a minor operation at a local hospital.

Scales' work is stored on glass negatives and is of a great clarity. He would have used a large wooden tripod camera, which was focussed by eye onto a rear screen before sliding the unexposed glass plates into the back of the device. Scales visited Brocton Camp and other New Zealand depots, principally Sling Camp near Bulford on Salisbury Plain some time in late 1917. He took many pictures, including his most important contribution to the record of the Chase; the only clear and detailed contemporary photograph of the Model of Messines, almost complete in the old H lines of the camp. The Turnbull Library in New Zealand now holds much of his work, with many of the pictures digitised and available to view online.

Brocton Camp 1918, now designated as the New Zealand Reserve Brigade training centre.

The photographs illustrate many of the features that would appear common to all camps. One of these is a picture of a squad of twelve men, training at Brocton Camp. They wear shorts with their uniform tunics and steel helmets, as the New Zealanders tended to do, with their rifles stood in stacks behind them. In the background can be seen the monotonous wooden huts. The parade ground has no prepared surface, indicating the hurriedness of its original construction. Another photo shows a group of bombing instructors, all sergeants or NCOs, with an officer in their midst. Instructors were experienced men taken from front line duties for a three-month spell. One of the collection's images shows a group of PT instructors in their white undershirts, and the crossed rifles and boxing gloves indicate that they are participating in man-at-arms type sports and training. The railway line in the background is probably the Tackeroo Railway that passed through Brocton Camp.

More intimately, there is a picture of at least twelve young soldiers in a wooden hut similar to those used at Brocton and Rugeley. They cluster around a central table and in the rear is their only source of winter heating; a small, central coal or coke fired stove. The photo was taken during the summer, as the room is bright and several of the men are in their army issue undershirts, although one or two are in full camp uniform complete with military belts. These barrack huts would hold about twenty men.

The official history comments that when the camp was taken over by the 5th Battalion it was mainly full of young British soldiers, 18 year old conscripts in Young Soldiers battalions forming the 5th Reserve Division, waiting to turn 19 and be eligible for service at the front. In September 1917, the 5th Battalion NZRB arrived with 1925 men, precisely noted as, although heavy drafts had recently been sent away to France *'the 27th Reinforcements had marched in some 10 days previously'*. The 5th Battalion seems to have had about 2-3000 men in training for the NZ Rifle Brigade. Each batch of new conscripts (by now New Zealand had also introduced conscription) was labelled consecutively 15th, 16th Reinforcements etc. They would now be sent from New Zealand around the world to Brocton, which by this time was known as the New Zealand Rifle Brigade Reserve Centre. World events were now impinging on Cannock Chase in no uncertain manner!

Once there, the men would have been put through training in preparation for front line duty. What we today regard as the unique feature of Brocton Camp and of great historic importance is the terrain model of Messines. This object communicated the 'topographical instruction' of the role of the Brigade and New Zealand Division in the taking of Messines village during the Battle of Messiness on 7th June 1917. Standing there overlooking the large concrete scale model of the village and the surrounding trench lines, the trainees would have heard the story of the assault and the pride of the NZRB in its achievement would have been drummed into them.

Terrain Models and The Battle of Messines

The 7th June 1917 saw one of the three most successful British and Empire attacks of the war, all of which lasted just one day

Squad of New Zealand trainees, in shorts, probably in the English Winter. Landmarks of tank and chimneys confirm this as Brocton Camp.

and achieved all their initial objectives. The first of these was the capture of Vimy Ridge by the Canadian Corps at the start of the Battle of Arras; the second was the storming of the Messines Ridge and the third was the breakout from Villers Brettoneux, on 8th August 1918, the first day of the end of the war.

The Battle of Messiness was planned as a necessary precursor to the Third Battle of Ypres, known as Passchendaele. Field Marshall Douglas Haig planned for an offensive in northern Flanders around Ypres with the aim of breaking through to the northeast and capturing Ostend and Bruges, the inland base of the North Sea U-boats that were waging unrestricted submarine warfare on any shipping within British waters. Prior to that, it was necessary to clear the enemy from their advantageous positions along the high ground of the Messines Ridge, south of Ypres, from where they could

Guard. Changing the guard at a New Zealand camp. The troops are in full pack and outdoor order with bayonets fixed.

observe the British lines and preparations within the Ypres Salient. The German Army had been in possession of the ridge since 1914 and was well dug in, accordingly the British faced an uphill attack against thoroughly prepared positions.

To combat this problem, the British had a surprise prepared for the attack. For over a year, tunnelling companies, the brainchild of an Empire adventurer and civil engineer turned soldier, Sir John Norton-Griffiths, had been tunnelling towards the German lines and strong points. As a result, 21 huge explosive mines had been laid along the front line from Hill 60, through St Eloi and down the line towards Peckham Farm and Spanbroekmolen. Each one was upwards of 75,000 lbs of explosive. The combined explosive power would almost equal the mega-ton effect of the first atomic bomb and until that event would be the largest man made explosion in history. Geologists had established that the ridge sat on a layer of sand deep within its base and it was further aimed that the explosion would 'earthquake' the ridge, causing massive vibrations and movements that would shake and collapse trenches and dug-outs and even overturn concrete pill boxes. The initial shock would be followed by a massive, well-planned creeping barrage that would lead and protect the troops upwards to the summit of the ridge and on into the ruins of Messines village itself.

Before the war Messines had had a large and prominent church, with a rounded dome that could be seen for miles around. By 1917, it lay in ruins, its crypt serving as a shelter for many German soldiers, including one infamous occupant who later recalled sheltering there: Corporal Adolf Hitler. In the centre of the attack zone in the middle of the ridge the task of seizing the ruins was allocated to the New Zealand Division. Preparation for the attack was meticulous. It was planned by General Hubert Plumer's Second Army as a

one-day 'bite and hold' operation, as opposed to the massive
month long offensives that had proved so costly before. Their
objectives were to turn out the enemy and then seize and hold
the Ridge.

Training for the battle: the Petit Pont terrain model
During the preparations for the battle troops were able to
familiarise themselves with the layout of the defences that
they would encounter as well as the ground's topography
and their own objectives. This was achieved via the building
of a large-scale military model that covered the whole ridge.
It was constructed behind the lines, close to the small village
of Romarin, a mile or so west of Ploegsteert, at a place called
Petit Pont. The actual site has not since been identified but
contemporary photographs exist of it. These images show the
model next to a straight stretch of road with a row of trees in
the distance. It was clearly close enough to be in range of the
enemy, as a shell can be seen exploding in the distance in one
of the photos. At least twice the size of its later progeny, the
Cannock Messines model, it is built either from crushed chalk
or light coloured soil. The same crenulated trenches as used in
the Cannock model can be identified and several points appear
to have small labels on them to mark positions or noticeable
features.

There is also a short film of Australian troops studying the
model, which can today be seen on You Tube, and a famous
publicity photograph shows the Australian hero, Captain
Albert Jacka VC, studying his maps against the model in front
of him. There was a walkway around the model and a raised
wooden platform where men could obtain an elevated view
of the area. In turn, all battalions taking part in the attack
were brought to Petit Pont and officers were free to attend
whenever they wished. Several official histories refer to the

model and visits by battalion and divisional troops, each there to thoroughly familiarise themselves with the topography of Messines as well as their attack route and objectives.

From the model at Petit Pont we can see where the NZRBs inspiration came from to create a similar model back at their Brocton training camp, something that could be used for the instruction and training of new recruits. The training battalion would have been aware of it and many of the instructors, men rotated back from front line service, would personally have seen it. Not only would it have been seen as an instructional tool but also as an inspirational way of explaining the recent history of the NZRB and its achievements at Messines.

On the morning of 7th June 1917, the attack began. At 3.10 am, nineteen tunnelling officers, spread out along the battlefront, studied their synchronised watches and simultaneously plunged the firing handles on their detonator boxes. One brushed his hand against an electric terminal and recalled being thrown flat on his back by the firing current. Another thought for a second that nothing was happening, that perhaps their firing circuit had broken, or the German pioneers opposite had broken into the mine and cut the wires or even removed the explosive. But a fraction of a second later the ridge began to shake and heave as a low rumbling began that seemed to get louder and louder until nineteen different mushrooms of earth rose skywards with red flames and gases bursting forth, hurling earth, debris and the bodies of men high into the air.

As the debris and remains fell back to earth and the huge columns of smoke and gas towered skywards, the British artillery barrage crashed out with a deafening roar. All along the front the British and Empire divisions were formed up. The Australian 3rd Division was on the right of the line with the New Zealand Division in the centre. On the left, divisions included the 36th Ulster and the 16th Irish, fighting side by side for the first time in the war. All went 'over the top', climbing out of their front line trenches and following the rolling barrage across No Man's Land and into the German trench system beyond.

Initially, there was little opposition as those Germans in the front line had either been killed or vaporised by the tremendous explosions under their lines. The survivors had indeed experienced the expected earthquake as their trenches rocked and shook throughout the conflagration. Many were wandering shaken and dazed and many willingly surrendered, but further back opposition began to stiffen. As the New Zealanders advanced further they came under machine gun fire from posts shooting through the advancing British barrage.

It was here that Lance Corporal Sam Frickleton of the New Zealand Rifle Brigade won fame and the Victoria Cross for an act of outstanding bravery. Seeing that machine gun posts were holding down his men and causing casualties, he ran forward, actually through the British barrage, and single-handedly knocked out two machine guns and their crew. His courage allowed the advance to continue and the immediate objective to be captured. He saved the lives of many of his comrades who would otherwise have been caught in the withering crossfire. Lance Corporal Frickleton survived the attack and was personally invested with the Victoria Cross by King George V at Buckingham palace the following September.

Within twelve hours the battle and advance had been a huge success. Although resistance continued to stiffen as the German command tried to infiltrate re-enforcements onto the crest of the ridge, the objectives, which had been in German hands since October 1914, were all taken, held and

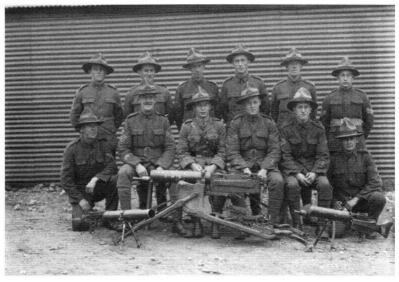

Machine gun training section at a New Zealand camp. The gun of the Left is the British Lewis light machine gun. The central gun is a captured German Maxim machine gun and tripod with a captured light machine gun on the Right.

reinforced as the new British front line. Casualties, by Great War standards, had been relatively light. The villages of Whytschaete and Messines on the summit of the ridge were all taken. With visual observation into the Ypres Salient now denied to the enemy the stage was set for the main preparations for the Third Battle of Ypres to begin. Sadly, that battle would deteriorate into a slogging match of attrition, bogged down in the liquid mud of one of the wettest late summers and autumns of the twentieth century. Nevertheless, its precursor had been an outstanding military success and the men of the New Zealand Division had played a major part in it.

The Brocton Camp Model of Messines
The New Zealanders took over responsibility for training at Brocton in mid 1917. They quickly established their own training routine. And fairly swiftly the decision was taken

to recreate the Petit Pont model as an aid for topographical instruction. However, there was more meaning to the model than just that. The Division and the NZRB were rightly proud of the part they had played in the battle. They had taken on the enemy and beaten them thoroughly, turning them out of their entrenched positions that had been in their hands for nearly three years. The aim of the model was also to enable reinforcements to gain a sense of pride and esprit de corps in the units they would be joining. Many of the training battalion would have seen the Petit Pont model and its method of construction using aerial photographs and maps would have been well known. Several features in common with each can be seen in photographs of the models. Trench lines were represented by zigzag (crenulated) patterns, in a similar manner to markings used on army trench maps. Straight lines represented roads and some were inlaid with pebbles to make them more prominent. The message was clear:

Here is where we fought, this is what we, the New Zealanders did and achieved.

The location of the model is interesting as it was built on the old H lines parade ground, suggesting that this area close to the PoW camp was now underused and possibly empty. The few pictures that exist reinforce this. The huts have an empty look with the doors wide open and windows bare. There is no evidence of men or occupation. The clearest photograph is by Tommy Scales and is crisp and well focused, showing the final stages of construction in great detail. Most interestingly, it appears to confirm local accounts mentioned in *A Town* that German PoWs physically constructed it. Two PoWs in their small round forage hats can be seen working within the fenced off area clearly labelled as '*Out of Bounds*'.

The picture shows that the area has been landscaped with a small raised part representing the ridge and the village of Messines is represented by block shaped houses with sloping concrete roofs. The church is depicted, not by a large domed building, as at Messines but as a typical English church complete with battlemented tower. Rumour has it that there was a large pocket watch embedded into the face that showed the correct time. Otherwise, the layout is believed to be an accurate representation of the trench lines guarding the access to the summit. A smooth concrete screed into which crenulated trench lines have been made covers the ground. So accurate was the model that when a small surviving section of it was uncovered in the 2008 archaeological survey, it could be recognised and correlated with a trench map of the time. The model appears to be surrounded by raised ground that would

The terrain model of Messines village under construction at Brocton Camp mid 1918. The notice states Out Of Bounds whilst two German prisoners can be seen lower Left working on its construction.

have allowed observation over the area while an instructor related the history of the attack.

The model remained in existence up to at least the start of the Second World War, gradually declining in condition throughout the late 1930s. Even while the remains of the camp were still in existence, a later photo, grainier and less well detailed, shows the model with grass and vegetation growing out of the trench lines. There is record of a local scout group being asked to carry our occasional maintenance on the site, weeding out such growth and keeping the trench lines clean of soil and vegetation. With the outbreak of the Second World War, visits to the sites ceased, falling leaves and vegetation covered the model and its location gradually became lost, until its re-location in the early 2000's.

The Importance of the Brocton Camp Messines Terrain Model

The site is at last being recognised as one of singular importance to our military history. As far as is known, it remains the only surviving example (in whatever condition it may prove to be) of an accurate semi-permanent terrain model from the First World War, constructed from contemporary records and more importantly, by men who must have taken part in the assault. At present, its future remains uncertain but with the approach of the centennial of the Great War the unique importance of the site is being increasingly recognised. At time of writing, in 2013, an announcement has been made regarding funding being achieved for an excavation to uncover, study and assess the remains and probably re-cover to ensure preservation for future generations.

CHAPTER 7

THE END OF THE WAR AND DEPARTURE

FOLLOWING THEIR success at Messines, the New Zealand Rifle Brigade still had nearly eighteen months of hard fighting before them. They remained within the Salient for the Third Battle of Ypres, which raged from July to November 1917. On an auspicious date, the 11th November, with exactly one more year of the war to run, the Canadians finally struggled up onto the top of the Passchendaele Ridge and captured the brick red stain in the muddy ground – all that was left of the pulverised village of Passchendaele. Both sides had now exhausted themselves in attack and defence, and winter was now upon them. Accordingly, Douglas Haig ordered the battle to be closed down and both sides consolidated themselves in their new positions and planned for further offensives in 1918.

At the start of yet another year of war the NZRB found themselves out of the line as Corps Reserves. From here, they were called south to the Somme area on March 23rd as the Kaiser's offensive crashed into General Gough's ill prepared and over stretched Fifth Army. It was a last and desperate attempt to break through and separate the British and French Armies before the Americans could tip the balance of the war permanently in favour of the Allies. The New Zealanders did sterling service plugging a large gap in the retreating line and preventing a possible break through and a rolling-up flanking movement.

The brigade was also fully involved in the final great allied offensive, the last 100 Days of the war, when the German Army was finally thrown back and subjected to unstoppable pressure all along the Western front. Their final action came a week before the war's end, as they stormed and took the French town of Le Quesnoy. The casualty figures show how desperate the fighting was:

	Killed	Wounded	Missing
Officers	6	13	-
Other ranks	37	238	-

It was a terrible price for the Brigade and New Zealand to pay; 43 killed and 251 wounded all in a single day's fighting, and just a few days before the war's end. News of the Armistice probably reached the 43 homes far away before they learnt of their loved ones' death in action.

On the morning of the 11th November came the communication everyone had waited four years for:

> *'Hostilities will cease at 11am. All units will stand on the line reached and await further orders. There will be no fraternisation with the enemy'.*

The war had reached its bitter end and the New Zealand Division initially marched to Cologne as part of the first occupying forces into Germany. From here, repatriation could begin as British Army units, such as the Brocton Young Soldiers battalions were moved in as garrison troops. Priority for demobilisation was given to those with low service numbers, i.e. early volunteers and married men. By mid 1919, most had returned home.

New Zealand paid a disproportionably heavy price in terms of men killed and wounded when compared to the other Empire Armies. 16,000 died and 40,000 were wounded up to the war's end; a heavy price for a small nation of around two million to pay. Her men rest in cemeteries along the Western Front and the names of her missing are carved in the walls of the Tyne Cot cemetery and the Butts and Messines Ridge cemeteries in Flanders as well as at Caterpillar Valley on the Somme. Away from the old frontlines, nearly seventy young men of the New Zealand Rifle Brigade rest in Cannock Chase Cemetery. The living went home with messages of good will for their future from both their Brigade and Divisional commanders. In assessing their contribution to Allied victory, it is perhaps instructive to quote a German intelligence assessment of the New Zealand Division found in the many enemy papers captured at the end of the war.

> *A particularly good assault division. Its characteristics are a very strongly developed individual self-confidence or enterprise, characteristic of the colonial British and a specially pronounced hatred of the Germans. The division takes pride in taking few prisoners.*

The Division had come from initial formation as a unit of no practical experience to being one of the crack colonial divisions of the British Empire. The army came to rely on them heavily, especially in the second half of the war, and the New Zealand Rifle Brigade were an intrinsic part of achieving victory. Brocton, as the New Zealand Rifle Brigade Reserve Centre, played an essential role in training reinforcements and forwarding them on as trained infantrymen, imbued with the fighting spirit of the division, to fill the never-ending requirement of replacements for their dead and wounded.

Its importance to the Allied war effort should not be underestimated and certainly not forgotten.

PART 2

CHAPTER 8

REMAINS ON THE CHASE TODAY

S URFACE ARCHAEOLOGY may often be disappointing to the casual observer. Some knowledge of what happened at a location, what existed there and a good imagination are generally helpful. Superficially, there are not many obvious remains of the Great War camps left. As previously stated, they were built on what is known as 'soft foundations', leaving not much of a footprint on the landscape. 'Harder' landscaping did take place and that may be useful in coordinating any remaining features with maps or plans of the site. This short guide will hopefully be helpful to the reader in identifying some of the remaining features and their significance.

The Visitor Centre and Original Great War Hut
Placed centrally on the Chase within the southeast corner of Rugeley camp, the Cannock Chase Visitor Centre is a modern brick building useful for its associated café facilities and adjacent toilet block. Within the shop is a display relating to RAF Hednesford and a book in which any visiting old RAF trainees are invited to sign and record their presence. The shop is a good outlet for amongst other things copies of the

Whitehead's book, *A Town For Four Winters* as well as leaflets issued by Staffordshire County Council on aspects of the Chase. Two of these are particularly relevant; *The Military use of the Chase* and *RAF Hednesford*.

Behind the visitor centre is the only large surviving artefact from the period of the Great War, an original training centre military wooden barrack hut. This is known to be so as it was purchased as surplus after the war to be a local parish room. After years of whist drives, parish dances, jumble sales, parish council meetings and so on, it was again declared surplus to requirements in the late 1990s. With some foresight and imagination it was offered to the visitor centre, where it was re-established on its present site. It has been accurately and imaginatively re-furbished, complete with metal beds, hut furniture and the small, totally inadequate stove that was the only source of heat. On one bed is a complete lay out of kit as if for inspection. It gives an idea of the large numbers of items of equipment that had to be provided for each soldier apart from uniforms and weaponry. The beds also shows how closely packed the huts were, a key cause of the spread of the influenza virus in 1918. Apart from anything else, no concession to privacy was made at all for the other ranks. Living was always in full view of one's fellow trainees. The hut also contains exhibits and information on the camps and an excellent model of the training centre's layout.

RAF HEDNESFORD

The visitor's centre and the Great War hut are situated in what was the northeast corner of the large RAF camp established there in the 1930s.

RAF Hednesford was not an aerodrome but a training and instructional centre for the essential engineering support staff to the RAF. Known as No 6 School of Technical Training, mechanics, riggers, airframe specialists, electricians, arm-ourers and all trades essential for the maintenance and serviceability of the front line fighting and transport strength would be schooled.

One of Hitler's ambitions following his rise to power in the mid 1930s was the creation, contrary to the 1919 Treaty Of Versailles, of a large and powerful air force, the Luftwaffe. Led by the Great War flying ace and former commander of Richthofen's Flying Circus, Hermann Goering, numbers of new and advanced aircraft began rapidly pouring out of German factories. Fast two engined bombers, Dorniers and Heinkels, the Stuka dive bomber for close army co-operation, and above all an advanced, all metal, single wing fighter, the Messcherschmidt 109, all threatened to give Germany a superiority over the aircraft available to the RAF at the time.

Finally, if rather belatedly, the country set about re-armament to face the forthcoming conflict that became inevitable after the many broken promises and the time won at Munich by Neville Chamberlain. Although the RAF lagged behind in modern bombers, the order of two new types of fighter aircraft; the Hawker Hurricane and the Supermarine Spitfire (the latter designed by Reginald Mitchell from nearby Stoke On Trent) came just in time and only just in sufficient numbers to ensure the 'Few' prevailed in the Battle of Britain during1940. Many of the ground crews and tradesmen that kept the fighters in the air had undertaken their training at RAF Hednesford.

By the end of the war, the RAF found itself with many more men than it required and Hednesford became one of its demobilisation, or de-mob, centres. Many airmen passed through to be officially signed off muster, released from service and sent back to 'civvy street' wearing one of the famous free de-mob suits, complete with civilian shoes, a hat and overcoat all provided by a grateful government.

By the early 1950s, in the face of an increasing Cold War threat, the services continued to fill their ranks by means of National Service, compulsory conscription of 18 year olds for two years military service in a branch of the Armed forces. Hednesford was chosen to become one of its five National Service initial training centres and in the course of six years over 80,000 recruits passed through, undertaking their eight week basic training course before being passed onto other centres. By now, RAF Hednesford was an extremely large camp. Much of the accommodation remained as wooden barrack huts but the site also boasted three churches. There was also a synagogue, the only one on a RAF camp, so all young Jewish recruits were automatically sent there for their training. There was also a camp cinema, sports facilities and of course the central feature, the large parade ground, which no one was allowed to set foot on unless under specific instruction to do so. The camp displayed several gate guardians including at different times a Hurricane and a Spitfire.

A friend, John Penny, local stalwart of the Birmingham Branch of the Western Front Association, undertook his basic RAF training at Hednesford in the early 1950s. As a young 18 year old arriving at the local station he remembers being disorientated and confused with red-faced NCOs yelling and screaming at him from the very first moment, no doubt all part of the process of moulding recruits into what the RAF wanted. The place was isolated, cold and bleak, described by John as probably being similar in organisation to the far away Stalag camps that many Allied PoWs had so recently endured. A local lad from Erdington, North Birmingham, John was later astonished to find out the camp was probably no more than 25 miles in a straight line from his home! To him, and probably most recruits from even further away, it must have appeared so isolated that it might as well have been in Siberia.

By 1956, the government was considering the abolition of National Service and looking to defence being provided by professional services, with the Territorial Army and other units in reserve. Finally, it was decided that RAF Hednesford would be surplus to requirements and due for closure. However, before that could be accomplished, once more events far away in Eastern Europe reached out to have an effect on the still isolated Chase.

In 1956, in Hungary, behind the Iron Curtain since the end of the Second World War and firmly within the grip of the Soviet Union, the populace rose up in a desperate effort to throw off Communist rule. Astonishingly, in the course of the summer months, the Hungarian people fought the para-military police and Russian forces to a standstill, particularly within the capital, Budapest. The Central Committee of the USSR seemed to accept the situation and appeared agreeable to a withdrawal of its forces, but two days later changed its mind and ordered a full invasion of Hungary by the Red Army. In vain, citizens' radio pleaded for help and even intervention by NATO and the Western powers. This was at the height of the nuclear standoff of the Cold War and the West would not risk escalation into a Hot War, even for such a deserving cause.

Many Hungarians fled abroad to escape the fighting and the inevitable retribution of the Soviet forces and secret police. A large number received asylum in Great Britain. As always, the problem was where to find emergency housing. Even ten years after the Second World War Britain was still struggling to replace its housing stock, much of which had been damaged in the war and large estates of pre-fab housing still existed around most major cities. RAF Hednesford, now empty and ready for disposal, was one of the sites chosen and so 4 or

500 refugees and their families received shelter there for a year while plans were made to allocate them accommodation elsewhere. Goodness knows what they must have thought of this cold and bleak winter upland. Perhaps better here and free than home under tyrannical rule?

By the end of 1957, the last of the refugees had moved on into more permanent and hopefully civilised accommodation. The camp was finally empty and, as with its predecessors of the Great War, it could at last be dismantled and buildings demolished. Once cleared, several sources mention the site was further flattened by a layer of local mining spoil being dumped and spread over it. Today, the grass has grown and trees are now seen across the site. Not much remains as topographical or archaeological information. But the main entrance on Marquis Drive, known as Kitbag Hill to so many inmates who struggled up and down that road to the nearest railway station, remains in-situ. From the map in the excellent leaflet available from the Visitor Centre one can orientate one self and perhaps even dare to walk onto the site of that forbidden parade ground!

CHAPTER 9

CANNOCK CHASE WAR CEMETERY AND THE GERMAN MILITARY CEMETERY

THE CANNOCK Chase War Cemetery is virtually unique in mainland Britain as being one of only perhaps four or five complete Commonwealth War Graves Commission (CWGC) military cemeteries set out within the UK.

The cemetery, like the others, conforms to the same layout and appearance as those in France and Flanders, and elsewhere across the continent and the world. Stand within it, look around and one could easily be persuaded one stood close to the Somme battlefield, or Ypres, or Passchendale. Similar small cemeteries can be found all along the old Western front. Unlike many church and civilian burial grounds, which may have single or small clusters of military CWGC graves scattered within them, Cannock is a purely military cemetery and has all the same features; rows of white Portland Stone headstones, all to the same pattern, the Cross of Sacrifice with the Crusader's Sword affixed to the top and surrounded by a beech hedge. At the base of the rows of headstones are flowers

View of Cannock War Cemetery, almost unique in Britain as a purely military, almost exclusively Great War cemetery.

and shrubs, planted, trimmed and cared for by the CWGC gardeners and work gangs.

The Imperial War Graves Commission changed after the Second World War to the Commonwealth War Graves Commission and this metamorphosis is an interesting story worthy of a few words. Its formation is generally held to be the culmination of work initiated by a 45-year-old, ex-newspaper editor who became a Major General, Sir Fabian Ware. Fabian Ware first went to war in 1914, not as a soldier but in command of an ad-hoc Red Cross ambulance unit, several of which were formed providing medical support to front line units. In 1915, the story goes that Fabian Ware stood in Bethune churchyard, studying the graves of some recently killed soldiers. It suddenly occurred to him that, as far as he knew, nobody was keeping any official or even unofficial records of these burials and their locations. After the war, relatives would presumably wish to know where their loved ones lay and so more permanent arrangements would have to be made to lay out and care for those cemeteries.

Ware made enquiries to the Red Cross and army and the Red Cross suggested that as Ware had raised the matter perhaps he would like to take the task on himself. It provided a small secretariat and work began, both visiting the front lines to record burials and seek chaplains' records, many of who conducted burial services for their men wherever possible. As the war went on and the scale of the fighting and numbers of dead increased beyond anything ever previously envisaged, Ware realised only the army had the resources to undertake this vast work. After lobbying, the War Office gave into requests, Ware was commissioned as an officer, a Graves Registration Unit was established and formal returns and records began to be kept. These would form the basis for the CWGC casualty database available online today.

In 1917, the Imperial War Graves Commission was proposed and charged with responsibility for the creation and maintenance of military cemeteries 'in perpetuity'. It would have Empire members from countries whose soldiers had fallen in the cause and the British and Empire governments, in proportion to the number of burials in each, would meet the costs. The IWGC was also charged with devising memorials to the missing, the nearly 50% of recorded fatalities whose bodies were never found or identified.

The Commission published for consultation the three principles on which their work would be based. Firstly, there would be individual remembrance. Wherever possible, each body known or unknown, would receive an individual burial and headstone. There would be no mass graves. The names of the missing would be recorded individually on a suitable memorial. Secondly, there would be equality of remembrance. Whatever their rank, social or military status each man was held to have made the same supreme sacrifice. Each would receive a uniform size headstone marked in a uniform pattern with a badge of their regiment or unit and individual details, with relatives able to provide two lines of epitaph or remembrance at the foot of the headstone. There would be no cross as such unless the stone was of an unknown soldier. Thirdly, and most controversially, there would be no repatriation of remains back to the United Kingdom. All men would remain either in cemeteries in their theatre of operation where first buried or be removed to a local concentration cemetery, for there were far too many small cemeteries to be properly maintained and cared for.

Surprisingly, these principles, when proposed, caused deep and bitter controversy. Many had thought to place their own headstone and memorial on their relative's grave. Many more, especially the wealthier in society, had hoped to bring the body home for burial in a local churchyard or cemetery where they could be seen and regularly visited. As always, one or two popular newspapers took up the cause of those opposed, supported by several members of the aristocracy and even a bishop or two. It took much public and political persuasion by Fabian Ware, supported by public figures such as Winston Churchill and Rudyard Kipling (who had lost his son at Loos) before an Act of Parliament could be successfully passed creating the legal status of the IWGC and enshrining its principles of operation.

So, in perhaps the finest example of these principles, in Warloy-Baillon Cemetery behind the Somme front is buried Major-General E.C. Ingouville-Williams, 'Inky-Bill' to his troops and one of the highest ranking British officers to be killed in the Great War. A general officer commanding the 34th Division, killed by a shell whilst visiting the Somme front line on 22nd July 1916, he lies with his men of all ranks beneath a stone of equal size and layout as that of the humblest Private.

Cannock Chase War Cemetery

The cemetery is laid out according to the Commission's principles. Visitors will be surprised to see that although an Imperial and latterly Commonwealth cemetery, the largest numbers of burials here are of German Prisoners of War; 350 in number. A smaller number of 90 Empire troops lie at the front and to the right of the entrance. Such is the preponderance of German burials that the cemetery was known as the 'German Cemetery' in the 1920s and 30s, although a few of the 350 are actually Second World War burials re-sited here to in-fill gaps when the German Cemetery was created at the end of the 1950s. The fact that the cemetery exists here at all is due to those commission principles. The vast majority of the Empire burials are young men of the New Zealand Rifle Brigade, most of them trainees here at the Reserve Centre. This was deemed to be both their area of operation and the no repatriation rule would therefore apply.

The Spanish Flu Epidemic of 1918

Looking at the headstones one thing becomes immediately obvious; the majority of Empire men are young, in their early twenties and probably at the peak of physical fitness. Most died in the five-month period of October 1918 to February 1919. The majority of German burials from the PoW camp are also in this time scale. The reason is the passage through the Midlands of the last great global pandemic of illness, the Spanish Flu, probably the worst and most widespread since the Black Death burnt its way across Europe and Britain in the 14th century.

The conditions were just right. For the first time there was industrialised mass movement of populations around the globe. Men from across Europe, the British Empire, Africa (French colonial troops) and India (the Indian Army contingent brought here by the British in 1914) had concentrated along a European battlefront and now several million Americans were also to be transported there. Both the British and French Governments had already moved huge numbers of Chinese labourers (the Chinese Labour Corps) to the Western Front. Even such an isolated place as Cannock Chase now housed large numbers of men from home and abroad: German prisoners and New Zealand and British soldiers. Residual populations elsewhere were undernourished as food priority went to the military. German and Russian civilian rations approached starvation levels. With so much of the world's population suddenly living in enforced close proximity, with resistance to disease low amongst whole populations, the scene was ripe for a terrifying worldwide pandemic.

The origin of the strain of Spanish Flu virus is not known but it is thought to have originated in America, probably amongst the vast training camps being set up to support the three or four million men promised to be available in France in 1918 and 1919. With their movement it spread both east-wards and westwards. It crossed the Pacific, devastating the populations of Pacific Islands and virtually depopulating places such as Samoa. In Europe, its existence was not publicised, as it was thought likely to be bad for morale. In any case, by autumn 1918, German resistance was at last collapsing, victory after victory was being won as the German Army retreated towards the Fatherland's borders and the newspapers were full of this exciting news. The flu was first extensively reported in neutral Spanish papers and these reports are where it acquired its name. Its most deadly effect appeared to be its high mortality rate amongst the younger, fitter members of society. It produced severe pneumonia type symptoms, where the younger victims quickly drowned in the extensive lung secretions the disease produced. It is estimated by various sources that more of the world's population died as a result of the pandemic than as a result of the fighting during the preceding four years.

The New Zealand military command was aware of the approaching problem and the official history records some of the preparations made. A section of huts were set-aside as an elementary isolation hospital and anyone showing symptoms was quickly isolated there. The first wave of flu appeared in the summer of 1918 but did not seem too virulent. Most men recovered. But in the autumn the virus appears to have mutated into a far stronger strain, which again passed through later in the autumn and this time caused multiple fatalities amongst local populations and within both the military and PoW camps.

Burials within the cemetery

As with any CWGC military cemetery, the details of the men and their backgrounds show the diverse cross section of society represented by the army later in the Great War. All of the larger cemeteries abroad have copies of the cemetery register behind a small brass door set near the entrance. The names of the men are listed in alphabetical order and usually there are some personal details of parents or wives. As at Cannock, some have no such details but merely have the regiment, battalion and date of death recorded. There are several like this at Cannock, presumably because no next of kin was known.

The New Zealanders are rather similar. Most are men in their twenties to thirties, with high army numbers, indicating they were probably reinforcements not long in Britain undergoing training before being sent onto France. Most give the usual personal details. By now the age of reinforcements was rising, most were in their late twenties and married. Cannock does not have a register on site but full details are available on the CWGC website.

One unusual casualty lies at Cannock. *Rifleman William Le Fleming, NZRB,* was in fact a member of the British aristocracy. He came from a branch of the British Le Fleming family who proudly traced their ancestry back to the Norman Invasion. Their family seat was Rydale Hall in Northumberland and William's father was Sir William Le Fleming 9th Bart. The family were settled at Rydale Manor, New Plymouth, New Zealand.

Another casualty demonstrates the horrible waste of life wrought by the Spanish Flu. One of only two officers buried at Cannock, *Lieutenant Cecil Blake* was a Doctor within the Royal Army Medical Corps and perhaps the most highly educated man within the cemetery, holding degrees both in law and medicine. Born in South Africa, he is typical of those Empire families who wished to support the Motherland's cause. Cecil was born in Burghersdorp South Africa. As a university student in South Africa he had already taken the triple qualification in Law before moving to Britain to further undertake training as a doctor in Edinburgh, where he obtained his MD. Cecil would have cared for men at Cannock before himself succumbing to the flu. He lies in row 4 G grave 14.

Another example of the Empire Spirit
Serjeant Charles William Allcock, 6th Battalion the Middlesex Regiment, also in row 4 G. Aged 44 on his death on 27/10/1918.
He is recorded as the husband of A V Allcock of Saskatchewan Canada. Many from the Dominions came to Britain to enlist

in the British Army rather than join fledgling Dominion forces and so were members of British Regiments. Presumably, Serjeant Allcock had been one such spirit, returning to the United Kingdom and being allocated to the Middlesex Regiment, probably on enlisting in London.

The youngest there

Boy Albert Urell, Royal Garrison Artillery, died 16/8/18 age 16.
Son of Henry and Laura Urell of Plymouth, Albert was a regular soldier granted the rank of Boy. Prior to the Great War, the army took on boys in their young teens that were usually trained as drummers. When they reached the age of 18 they could rise to Private and become a regular soldier. Albert must have signed on and spent time here in the Young Soldiers battalions. The date of death is early but he may have been an early victim of the generally less virulent first wave, of the Spanish Flu. Although parents' names are given we do not know if they were still alive, many boys enlisting were orphans. Anyway, nobody in Britain seems to have claimed his body, so he lies here amongst comrades.

And the oldest

Private Arthur Roberts, Labour Corps, died 19/11/1917, aged 48.
As the British Army took over an ever growing section of the Western Front so it requirements for labour grew proportionately. This demand was immense. Trench lines had to be dug and all building materials such as timber, iron sheeting and sandbags, all had to carried up to the line. Roads had to be laid and maintained, trench railways built, supplies loaded and unloaded. Almost every conceivable duty had to be done by human effort. The demand caused the formation of the Chinese Labour Corps where British and French governments recruited a large numbers of Chinese to be

brought to the Front for that purpose. But even that wasn't enough and the Labour Corps was formed for soldiers too old or unfit for front line duty. Battalions were also sent back to the UK particularly to undertake agricultural work, as most men had been conscripted away from the land. Arthur may have been one of these. Well above the average age, he may even have been a regular deemed too unfit, or perhaps it was as a result of wounds from front line service. Arthur died in 1917 well before the dates of the Spanish Flu, so possibly from natural causes.

The Polish Resettlement Corps

Stand in front of the Cross, with all the headstones facing you, turn to the right and follow the edge of the bushes around and you will come across a single isolated headstone from just after the Second World War; a Sergeant of the Polish Resettlement Corps. Following the German invasion of Poland in September 1939 many Poles escaped and came to Britain to take up the fight against the Germans. Polish squadrons within the RAF became famous and the Polish Division fought on may battlefronts in Africa and Europe. But at the war's end, Poland was firmly within the Soviet sphere behind the Iron Curtain. Many Polish servicemen felt they could not return home, as their lives would be in danger. Britain was willing for many to stay on and to facilitate their transfer into civilian life the Polish Resettlement Corps was formed. Servicemen remained under military discipline while housing and employment was sought for them. Hence the Sergeant's military rank and burial as a still serving soldier here whilst awaiting official demobilisation. As with others, he lies far from home but is a reminder of the Polish determination to be free, an aspiration that finally became real after the struggle of Solidarity during the 1980s.

The Cannock Chase German Cemetery was constructed in the early 1960s to bring in burials of German, servicemen and civilian internees, died in both World Wars, from scattered sites throughout the British isles.

The German Cemetery

A five-minute walk along the road to the side of the CWGC cemetery will bring you to the Cannock Chase German Cemetery. Its presence there is perhaps a little puzzling, as it has no connections with military activity on the Chase in either war. By the end of the Second World War, the graves of German service personnel, as well as internees from both wars, were scattered in multiple small or individual plots across the UK. In the 1950s, the West German government requested land for the construction of a single concentration cemetery where the bodies could be brought and where the ground, headstones etc could all be maintained in an appropriate and dignified manner. As mentioned earlier, a plot next to the CWGC cemetery would be ideal as they could be contracted to maintain the site. And some say there is a central Germanic air to this wooded portion of the Chase. So construction, exhumation and re-interment were carried out throughout the early 1960s.

Today, you enter by a doorway through an entrance hall. In the central area, lying supine, is a statue of a fallen soldier, wrapped in a cloak giving the impression of a fallen knight. To the right is the entrance to a small open area containing the grave markers of the four German air ship crews shot down over southern and eastern England in 1916.

It is now rather shocking to appreciate how early in the Great War the Zeppelin bombing of London began. In May 1915, only some nine months after the war began, the huge gas filled, canvas sheathed dirigibles, strengthened by wooden or aluminium frameworks and powered by motor driven propellers, appeared over London, bombing the civilian population below. These events caused something approaching panic amongst the population, further enhanced by the fact there seemed no defence against the menace. Searchlights could illuminate them but guns seemed unable to touch them. For the first time, Royal Flying Corps aircraft and pilots were re-called from the front and required to undertake night flights, something no aviator had ever attempted up to that point. Even if located, pilots reported that their standard armament of 303 ammunition seemed to have no effect on the huge craft. Well into 1916, German air ships, including the well-known Zeppelins, seemed to operate almost with impunity over the British capital. But in the summer of 1916, the British pilots decided to try a new tactic, loading the drums of their Lewis machine guns with three different types of bullets; ordinary .303 to puncture the gas bags, tracer to assist with aiming and an incendiary type explosive bullet, that hopefully would ignite the flammable hydrogen gas which all German airships were filled with.

On the night of the 3rd September 1916, a German air ship, SL 11, manufactured by the Schutte-Lanz company, took off with others for a mission over the north of London. This was not officially a Zeppelin as it was made by a different company and was shorter with a wooden frame, four engines and a smaller crew of 16. During the evening it reached and bombed St Albans in Hertfordshire. Operating from Sutton Farm, as a pilot of 39 Squadron, was Lieutenant William Leefe-Robinson, Worcestershire Regiment, attached as a pilot to the Royal Flying Corps and now recalled for Home Defence. With an air raid alert on and at least one Zeppelin spotted in the area Leefe-Robinson took off in a primitive BE2C night fighter. Gaining height, he eventually spotted an airship illuminated by searchlights. But in trying to get above the craft he, and probably the searchlights, lost track of it proving how immensely difficult it was to locate and maintain contact with these large flying monsters in the night sky.

Continuing the patrol, he again found an airship illumi-nated, now known to be SL11. Mindful of his previous experience this time he did not attempt to get height above it but closed directly on the enemy. With him he had three drums of ammunition. Getting close to the dirigible he fired two drums of ammunition at it, receiving return fire from guns on the airship, but there was no noticeable effect upon its structure or progress. Lying off to change over to his third drum of ammunition, Leefe-Robinson then tried a new tactic. Instead of raking the length of the airship he closed with the rear and this time fired long sustained bursts at a single point.

For a minute it seemed that this also had little effect, until to his elation, Leefe-Robinson observed a red glow behind the canvas covering. The hydrogen gas was igniting! Flames burst through the canvas skin and quickly spread along the length of SL 11 until it fell like a flaming meteorite, plummeting into the ground near Cuffley. With it perished the commander, Hauptmann Wilhelm Schramm and his entire crew of 15 men. The flaming fall of the airship was seen for miles around, even as far south as central London where it is said large crowds rushed out into the streets to witness the spectacle, cheering and singing Rule Britannia.

For his act of bravery, Lt Leefe- Robinson was awarded the Victoria Cross. He continued flying, but was shot down and captured in 1917. His time in captivity, a time of great deprivation and almost starvation for British prisoners, weakened him terribly. He was repatriated at the war's end, but in his weakened state succumbed, as with the Cannock New Zealanders, to another wave of the Spanish Flu on the last day of the last year of the Great War, 31st December 1918. Hauptmann Schramm and his crew were originally buried at Potters Bar, but with three other crews were later re-located to Cannock as the cemetery approached completion.

A similar fate befell the crews of the other three air ships. Their three craft; L32, L31 and L38 were all true Zeppelins manufactured by the Zeppelin Company rather than the Schutte-Lanz works. They were much larger with an aluminium framework, carried a larger volume of gas giving greater lift and allowing a larger crew, six engines and a greater bomb load. They also had a corresponding larger fuel capacity and so greater range. But all had the same deadly weakness; the flammable hydrogen gas needed to lift and float the craft in the air, for Germany had no access to neutral helium. Thus, in due course these three giants and their crews all suffered the same fate as SL11. From each there were no survivors. If a Zeppelin was set on fire there was no possible escape for the crewmen. The choice was terrible, as parachutes were not issued to airship crews so it was either stay and be incinerated in the flaming wreck, or jump.

By the end of 1917, a new weapon to carry the air war to London was ready, a high altitude twin-engine bomber, the Gotha. Now aeroplanes could fly direct to their targets no longer at the mercy of wind and weather. From then on, the Zeppelin airships were withdrawn from operations over London. Their job was done. Official figures list 557 civilians as having died in the raids with 1358 injured. More damaging to the war effort, several fighter squadrons had to be brought back from the Western Front to form the basis of a Home Defence system.

The Main cemetery

Passing back through the main hall into the main part of the cemetery reveals it to lie in two sections on the banks of a central small valley. Immediately closest are the Second World War burials. Ahead is an area of flattened stones, also Second World War and mostly in groups of three, killed on the same date. These are Luftwaffe aircrews brought down over England. On the far side of the valley are the burials from the First World War. The ranks are different here retaining the names of the old Imperial German Army, for instance Musketeer is quite common. Many of the soldiers belong to reserve regiments. Germany maintained a large standing army but every fit male undertook two years training and service in the army, remaining on the reserve with annual re-training for many years afterwards. By such means, once mobilisation was underway, Germany could field an army of three or four million trained men in a short time. Other categories are of interest, too. Internees are quite common in both world war plots. In both wars German civilians were felt to be a potential threat to National Security and many were rounded up for internment, ending up in commandeered boarding houses, surrounded by barbed wire, on the Isle of Man. Details of individual burials are not available on-line but individual queries can be addressed to the cemetery guardian.

Two very unusual burials lie within the ranks of the Second World War headstones. The majority buried here either died of wounds following capture or illness, or of natural causes during captivity. Some were recovered from downed aircraft, or were sailors washed up on the shore. However, two Second World War PoWs who lie in this cemetery, *Gerhardt Retting* and *Sgt-Major Wolfgang Rostberg*, were both deliberately killed, murdered in separate incidents in different camps, by fellow prisoners, as both were suspected of being informers. Following separate trials, five of Rostberg's and two of Retting's fellow PoWs, all hard line Nazis, were convicted and later hanged in Pentonville prison in London.

There also are two high-ranking officers. One an SS general and the other the highest rank of all, a Field-Marshall. Both were captured at the end of the war and both died of natural causes shortly afterwards. Both also share a similar history, one common to most high-ranking officers of the army of the Third Reich. Both were professionals, both in their younger service served throughout the Great War on the Western Front, winning medals for bravery and yet experiencing the pain and bitter humiliation of the defeat by the allies and the chaos and turmoil within their country in the 1920s. Both remained within the reduced army allowed under the Treaty of Versailles, then served in the expanding Wermacht as the new Nazi government increasingly ignored its treaty obligations in the late1930s.

SS General Maximilian Von Herff

Born in 1893, Von Herff was a young regular officer in the Imperial Army in 1914. He fought with distinction on the Western Front, rising to the rank of Colonel and decorated with the Iron Cross, both Second and First class. Remaining in the Wermacht, he was involved in France in 1940, then in North Africa where he commanded a battle group under Field Marshall Erwin Rommel. Again distinguishing himself, especially at the capture of Tobruk, he was made a Knight of the Iron Cross in 1943. A year earlier, he had formerly joined the Nazi Party and was later commissioned into the Waffen SS where he became an SS General. He was known to have been in Warsaw at the time of the Warsaw Ghetto uprising and to have been involved in inspections of concentration camps, such as Auschwitz. Made head of the SS Personnel Section, he reported directly to the head of the SS, Heinrich Himmler. The Personnel Section kept the records of all members of the SS and in effect spied on their own members, constantly assessing their loyalty and reporting to Himmler.

Captured at the end of the war, Von Heff was a PoW at Calderdale Hall, where he died apparently of natural causes on September 6th 1945. As a committed Nazi and high ranking SS officer who reported directly to the head of the SS, it is likely Von Herff would have faced war crime charges at Nurembourg and possibly even a death sentence if convicted for conniving in the dreadful Final Solution. Perhaps natural causes cheated Albert Pierrepoint, the official British hang-man, of another victim of justice.

Field Marshall Ernst Busch

Ernst Busch was born in 1885, joining the mainstay of German Imperial power, the Prussian Army, in 1904. As with Von Herff, he had a distinguished Great War, also being awarded the Iron Cross First and Second class. He was wounded and in 1918 was awarded the Pour Le Meritie. Staying on in the reformed Wermacht, he was promoted Lt-Colonel in 1930. He took part in the invasion of Poland in 1939 and operations across France during 1940. He was also awarded the Knight's Cross of the Iron Cross.

By 1941, he had risen to command the 16th Army in Operation Barbarossa (the invasion of Russia) fighting up to and taking part in the Siege of Leningrad. His army suffered a shock defeat by the Russians in June 1944, whereupon he was removed from command on Hitler's orders. However, in March 1945 he was brought back and given command of Army Group North West to try and halt the Allies attack from the west. By now, this was a hopeless task and he surrendered to Field Marshall Bernard Montgomery on 3rd May 1945. Brought back to the UK and initially lodged at Aldershot, he died of natural causes on the 17th July 1945.

So, on a rather bleak Staffordshire moorland, lie men from both sides of the two great conflicts of the twentieth century, all of who act as a permanent reminder of the century's conflicts and the sacrifice they required. From the humblest, a 16-year-old boy soldier, to the highest, a Field-Marshall, they now rest in peace.

CHAPTER 10

KATYN WOOD AND THE SITE OF BROCTON CAMP

The Katyn Wood Memorial

Further along the road, up a short access road opposite the tearoom, is the Katyn Wood Memorial. The memorial, placed here by an Anglo-Polish Friendship Society, commemorates the mass murder, now known to have been ordered by Joseph Stalin. Despite the fact that Russia was an ally during the Second World War, Britain might have ended up at war with her over Poland in1939. Whilst the German invasion of Poland in September 1940 was the act that brought Britain into the war, it is often forgotten that this treacherous act was compounded by a secret agreement made between Germany and the USSR, whereby the Red Army invaded the eastern half of Poland and Germany the west. Soviet forces and secret police were quick to round up the leadership of Polish society, not just military officers, but also as many members of the intellectual and professional classes. Doctors, lawyers, university lecturers, teachers, musicians and most of the upper strata of Polish society were taken into custody. In order to destroy that society orders were given for their murder and an estimated 22,000 were shot and buried in mass graves at Katyn

Wood and the surrounding areas, just inside the western edge of Russia. When the German invasion occupied this area, locals gave them information about the horrors in the Wood. The Germans were quick to recognise the propaganda value of this discovery and were as quick to excavate the site, filming and publicising the recovery of bodies, releasing the pictures to the world, citing this as an example of the barbaric nature of the Soviets.

The Soviets were equally as quick to muddy the waters by counter-claiming that, in fact, the Germans themselves had carried out the executions and were now pretending to discover the graves and use that as anti-Russian propaganda. This was despite the fact that Katyn Wood was, and always had been, within Russian territory prior to Operation Barbarrossa. The Polish government in exile and the Polish people after the war were in no doubt whom they blamed; the USSR. It was not until a brief period of Glasnost in 1990, under President Yeltsin, that records were finally made available and the then Russian Government admitted to the crime having indeed been carried out by Soviet forces on Stalin's orders.

The current memorial at Cannock is a reminder of the horror of the time. If one is visiting the National Memorial Arboretum, 20 miles east at Alrewas along the A38, then viewing the wonderful new Polish Forces Memorial there would be a good addition to the history of the Polish people in their struggle for existence and freedom.

The Site of Brocton Camp

Return from the Katyn memorial to the main road, turn right and then take the second small road on the right with a tarmac surface and follow this along. As the road bends left, in the grassland ahead can be seen the remains of some concrete structures. These were old coal hoppers where fuel was unloaded for the Tackeroo Railway, which ran straight across from left to right behind these remains. Follow the road up, parking on the left and cross the road to find the Glacial Boulder mounted on a plinth. The Boulder is part of an ancient natural history. It is granite and geologists identify it as originating in Scotland. Over the course of an Ice Age, for about 10,000 years, it slowly travelled southwards inside a glacier. Finally, a warmer age dawned, the glaciers melted and retreated and such anomalies as this were deposited where they fell.

The plinth stands on a large rectangular concrete base. Within that base are multiple cut-off steel stanchions firmly set into the concrete. As already mentioned, little hard surface archaeology remains, but here is proof that you are now standing within the heart of Brocton Camp itself. This is the base of the giant water tower tank, raised on steel stanchions and visible in many photographs of the camp.

Stand facing the Boulder. Many huts were situated behind you on the far side of the road, now mainly overgrown by scrub. To your left was the main ordnance and delivery store. Go past the boulder and up the slight bank straight ahead. You are looking down into what was clearly a railway cutting, now with trees growing within it. The Tackeroo main line ran on the far side but this as cutting for a branch leading up to the main store. Here the steam locomotives kept for hauling goods wagons would noisily have climbed up here, in clouds of steam and smoke, bringing all the necessary requirements up to the unloading bays in the stores.

Nearby were also the main cookhouse and bakery. A Tommy Scales' photograph shows the inside of a camp cookhouse with eight large oven ranges in a row and several large cauldrons for stews and soups. Around the room are various work surfaces. Close by was probably a butchers shop for dividing up carcasses. Photos of the bakery show men carrying huge two-man trays piled with loaves but also rudimentary camp ovens where men were trained in bakery under field service conditions.

Further hut lines are found a quarter of a mile up the road and can be found by looking for the not-very-obvious signposts to 'Freda's Grave' or even just 'FG'. At Freda's grave, complete with its new headstone, you are within the old H lines of the camp. Looking right and left it is possible to still make out that you are within one of the roadways of the camp, with some of the base brick work and hut platforms more easily visible here than opposite the Boulder.

Freda was the mascot of the New Zealand Rifle Brigade. Described in most sources as a Dalmatian, because she was black and white, photos show her instead to be a Great Dane. Legend has it she was found in France and sent back here but it is possible she may have been rescued locally. She was fondly

Headstone on Freda's grave. Freda was the Great Dane mascot of the New Zealand Rifle Brigade.

thought of and when she died before the war ended she was buried with a marker on her grave that was recently renewed by the Friends of Cannock chase. Her collar was taken home to New Zealand at the war's end and now resides in the New Zealand National Army Museum.

The site of the Messines Model lies behind the grave at an angle of about two o'clock and twenty yards distant. It is hard to identify unless its location is known but it is there, surrounded by a bank on three sides and a rather brambly central mound that once represented the village of Messines on its Ridge. The PoW camp is likely to have been on the far side of the parking area.

CONCLUSION

THE FIRST sixty years of the twentieth century were turbulent times. Nearly ten years of that period was spent waging world war. The century opened with Britain at war with the Boer settlers and farmers in South Africa.

It was old-fashioned warfare played out over vast areas of savannah by infantry and mounted troops. The horse was still the main source of power and transport. The Great War saw the industrialisation of warfare, the increasing power of the machine gun and artillery and the development of military aviation, all things taken forward and developed during the Second World War. Mechanisation in the shape of tanks and armour, air power and artillery came to dominate the battlefield. Then came the development and use of the atomic bomb, provoking its own period of Cold War, as the nuclear armaments of both sides led to an uneasy standoff.

The result was a profound revolution in the way the world was organised. Empires and Emperors fell and were swept away. The Kaiser of Germany, the Tsar of Russia, the Austro-Hungarian Empire, the Ottoman Empire, all fell and broke up into constituent pieces. From this emerged a second titanic struggle, one that reshaped the map of Europe and the world again. During it all the British Empire faded away and new power blocks were shaped and arose.

That these events should cause ripples at Cannock Chase now seems almost impossible. Look today at the open moorland and there are few physical remains to tell the story of what happened here. Yet for those with a little interest, traces of the history can be found. Some, like the Cannock Chase War Cemetery are permanent, as is a railway cutting in the hillside and the concrete base of the giant water tower. Most are fairly ephemeral; traces of hut outlines on the soil, faint track ways and old zigzag practice trench lines. Resting not far underground a model of a battle far off and long ago, built with pride by the men for whom participation in that battle and war on the Western Front was the fulfilment of a sacred duty to Homeland and their King.

Many men passed through this military area of the Great War. We do not know how many, but the inevitable result is that for many thousands this must have been their last spell in England before leaving for the Western Front. Spare them a thought. There many remain to this day, either as a known burial or a body found but unidentified, or perhaps not recovered at all, still within the soil of France or Flanders. The latter have not the honour of a named headstone, but each name is recorded, inscribed on one of the many memorials that grace the old British front lines. For many more the result was terrible wounds, possibly with a lifetime of disfigurement and disability. Faint whispers indeed, but stand at the glacial boulder, listen hard for those far off murmurings and think, 'If I was here a hundred years ago…."

We will remember them.

SOURCES CONSULTED, FURTHER READING AND INFORMATION

THE MAINSTAY of information on Brocton and Rugely camps for the past thirty years has been *A Town For Four Winters* by CJ and GP Whitehouse. Little else has been published on the subject since, either as a book or journal article. As the Great War has faded from human memory in terms of direct personal participation, so there is now no one left alive who experienced life, or training in the camps. With an essentially soft site in terms of archaeological features, knowledge of what occurred here for the thousands of soldiers who participated in the conflict has also began to slip away.

Information on the sites is now mainly found on the Internet, usually in short paragraphs and sections. This book is intended to set events at Cannock in their historical context and also as a basic guide to give some understanding as to what occurred. It is not intended as a detailed and academically referenced history of either of the sites or the military units involved. Research consisted mainly of collecting, collating and interpreting information from a range of Internet sites, official histories and other sources to build up the bigger picture. For readers who may wish to delve more deeply, I list below some of the sites and sources where information may be found in greater detail.

Christopher John, author.

SOURCES

History of the Camps and remaining features
Websites
STAFFS PAST TRACK: Website with historical and archaeological information. www.staffspasttrack.org

CANNOCK CHASE HERITAGE TRAIL: Details of walk through the Chase following sites of interest associated with the camps. www.cannockchasedc.gov.uk

CANNOCK CHASE MILITARY RAILWAY: An excellent site with details of the route of the Tackeroo railway through Brocton Camp. www.mrweb.co.uk

RAF HEDNESFORD: Website giving the history of RAF Hednesford, particularly for those who undertook National Service Training there. Contains a good gallery collection. www.rafhednesford.org

Official Histories
These may be accessed on line via The New Zealand Electronic Text Collection (NZETC): http://nzetc.Victoria.ac.nz

Especially the sections on: The Official History of the New Zealand Effort in the Great War, in particular Volume II: The New Zealand Division 1916-1919 by Colonel Hugh Stewart.

The Official History of the New Zealand Rifle Brigade especially Chapter 8: The Battle of Messines, and Appendix III: The New Zealand Rifle Brigade Training Battalion.

Photographs

The original camp photos are from the larger body of Thomas Frederick Scales' work on life in New Zealand camps in England, held by and available on-line at The Royal New Zealand Returned and Services Association Collection, Alexander Turnbull Library, Wellington New Zealand. Mp.natlib.govt.nz. Especially Mp.natlib.govt.nz/detail/?id=76884&l=en the picture of the Brocton model of Messines.

BIBLIOGRAPHY

A Town for Four Winters: Great War Camps of Cannock Chase by CJ and GP Whitehouse (ISBN 0 90297403 3).

Pillars of Fire: the Battle of Messines Ridge 1917 by Ian Passingham. The History Press (ISBN-10 075092540 X).

Messines Ridge by Peter Oldham, Battleground Europe, Pen and Sword books (ISBN-10 085052648).

Kitbag Hill: The Story of RAF Hednesford by C J Whitehouse (ISBN 0 9512903 0 4).